LAMBDA LITERARY AWARDS ◉ *Finalist.*
RAINBOW BOOK AWARDS ◉ *Honorable Mention.*

EXTRAORDINARY ADVENTURES
OF
MULLAH NASRUDDIN

*Naughty, unexpurgated tales of the beloved wise fool
from the Middle & Far East.*

REVISED EDITION.

collected & retold by RON J. SURESHA
Author, THE UNCOMMON SENSE OF THE IMMORTAL MULLAH NASRUDDIN.

NOTICE:

This book contains many old, bawdy, ribald tales
that explicitly explore taboo themes inappropriate for children.

MATURE READERS ONLY

will be amused and amazed by this unadulterated account
of the truly *Extraordinary Adventures of Mullah Nasruddin.*

Extraordinary Adventures
of
Mullah Nasruddin

*Naughty, unexpurgated stories
of the beloved wise fool
from the Middle & Far East*

Revised Edition

◉

Collected & Retold by
Ron J. Suresha

Bear Bones Books
New Milford, CT

Extraordinary Adventures of Mullah Nasruddin:
Naughty, unexpurgated stories of the beloved wise fool from the Middle and Far East

Revised edition, by Ron J. Suresha

Published by Bear Bones Books
137 Danbury Road #123, New Milford, CT 06776-3428
www.bearbonesbooks.com ~ bearsoup@gmail.com
First edition, Lethe Press, 2014. Revised edition, February 2018.

ISBN-13: 978-1-98205-567-7 ~ ISBN-10: 1-98205 -567-7

Design: Ron Suresha / Bear Bones Books
Cover illustration: Jaxinto

Library of Congress Cataloging-in-Publication Data

Suresha, Ron Jackson.
Extraordinary adventures of Mullah Nasruddin : naughty, unexpurgated stories of the beloved wise fool from the Middle and Far East / collected and retold by Ron J. Suresha.
    pages cm
    [ISBN-13: 978-1-98205-567-7 ~ ISBN-10: 1-98205 -567-7]
Includes bibliographical references.
    1. Nasreddin Hoca (Anecdotes) 2. Nasreddin Hoca (Legendary character)--Humor. I. Title.
    PN6231.N27S865 2014
    398.20956'02--dc23   2014033574

Contents

⊙

Extraordinary Adventures of Mullah Nasruddin

Part I
Mullah's Amazing Adventures

Part II
Young Nasruddin

PART III
Extra-Marital Affairs

PART IV
Meet the Nasruddins

PART V
Donkey Tales & Animal Crackers

PART VI

Adventures around the Village

PART VII

Travels with the Mullah

Forewarning

Salaam, dear Adult Reader:

Welcome to the thoroughly revised and partly redesigned edition of my second, and final, collection of Nasreddin Hoca folk humor, which includes many adult story topics, some of which are certain to offend, repulse, or trigger everyone.

As in my previous collection of Nasreddin Hoca folklore, *The Uncommon Sense of the Immortal Mullah Nasruddin* (Lethe, 2011), every single story included in its sequel, this volume, *Extraordinary Adventures of Mullah Nasruddin,* is entirely authentic, taken from published works listed in the Sources at the end of the book.

That said, the mature reader is hereby warned that some taboo topics of the 275 tales within this collection include: bestiality, animal cruelty, scatology, ethnic prejudice, racism, sexism, domestic abuse, marital infidelity, bigamy, homosexuality / bisexuality, transvestism, sodomy, pederasty, pedophilia, incest, blasphemy, apostasy, treason, violence, torture, homicide, war, and death.

The adult reader is advised, therefore, to prepare to be shocked and offended. If you read the book and care to share an unusual Mullah story not included here, please email me: mullahnasruddin@gmail.com or comment on the blog at MullahNasruddin.com.

To the parent or librarian:

If the reader knows and understands the meaning of the word *unexpurgated,* as in the subtitle to this book — *Naughty, unexpurgated stories of the beloved wise fool from the Middle and Far East* — the reader is certainly mature enough to read on. Otherwise, strict adult supervision is strongly advised.

The reader is cautioned of the inappropriateness of this book for children.

Preface

Coming from an ethnically diverse family with rich oral and literary folklore traditions, I became well acquainted early on with the stories of the famous folk character, Mulla Nasaruddin, a simple man of renowned humor and inscrutable wisdom, known for more than eight centuries in his native land as Nasreddin Hoca.

Sometimes my mother would tell a joke or story about the "wise fool" Nasaruddin (as he is called in Jewish folklore), usually to make a point about my contrary behavior. She would ask, for instance, "Why do you always answer a question with another question?" to which I could be reliably predicted to retort, "Oh really, do I?"

In my twenties, while living in several ashram (residential yoga center) communities in the U.S.A. and India, my teachers and fellow students would often tell, with great relish and humor, Sheikh Nasruddin "wisdom stories" as part of our regular lessons and lectures on spiritual life.

For more than two decades, Sufi writer Idries Shah's collections of Mullah Nasruddin stories were my only sources in English. Then, in 1999, while on my first trip to Istanbul, I acquired five Turkish-published volumes of Mullah stories in English, which were illustrated with cartoon tableaux depicting the adulterated punch-line moments from the most popular stories. Shortly after, I began to discover additional Nasreddin Hoca folklore sources online.

While compiling the first book, *The Uncommon Sense of the Immortal Mullah Nasruddin,* I volunteered to help reorganize the storybook collection of the Connecticut

13

Storytelling Center in New London, where I encountered several antiquarian Nasreddin volumes in various languages. Since then I have continued to gather and collate printed books and manuscripts in English, Hebrew, Spanish, German, French, Turkish, and Hindi, as well as material published online, all of which is included in the Sources following the text of this work.

The revised 2013 edition of *Uncommon Sense* is an anthology of more than 365 authentic individual stories, anecdotes, jokes, jests, and quips arranged biographically into seven parts with seven sections of seven stories each. While undoubtedly many pieces could be considered bawdy, abusive, or ethnic, the material was generally suitable for a collegiate adult readership, including hundreds of stories entirely appropriate for children. Sgott Mackensie's watercolor cover illustration of the bewhiskered, turbaned Mullah, happily riding his beloved donkey backward in a rural setting, reflected the book's broad appeal and presented it as a PG-13 collection appropriate for teenagers with parental guidance.

The positive critical reviews to the first book made it absolutely clear, however, that a second volume featuring the R- and X-rated material would be a welcome addition not just to Nasreddin Hoca scholarship but also to world literature. This turned out to be, to nobody's surprise except my own, a project requiring another five years of part-time independent scholarship.

While researching the topic of taboo humor, I discovered, in *The Horn Book* by folklore and humor scholar Gershon Legman, his stark condemnation of folk story and joke collections with all the bawdy or "objectionable" material expunged, which he calls "fakelore." Despite my earnest efforts to locate such risqué stories with limited success, I naturally cringed at the implication that I had unwittingly committed some sort of literary and folkloric misdeed by excluding the naughty and nasty tales of my old friend, Mullah Nasruddin.

Given the immense volume of this character's folklore, I was perplexed by the conspicuous absence of adult-themed stories among the hundreds I had indexed. The dearth of racy, earthy, profane, or ethnic material in the existing published folklore available to me seems due in part to its exclusion from popular children's presentations of the often-moralizing Mullah. My theory is that these "naughty Nasreddin" narratives were expurgated and adulterated from popular representations of Nasreddin in order to "reform" the character, according to the moral codes imposed first by Islamist and Turkish nationalistic influences, and later filtered through Victorian morality by English anthologists such as Shah and Barnham.

German Nasreddin scholar Ulrich Marzolph's analysis, "What Is Folklore Good For?" asserts that "Early Turkish manuscripts comprised a large amount of sexual, scatological, and otherwise disputable material" about the "vigorous and vulgar" Mullah. With that concept in mind, I delved even deeper into scholarly texts in search of this taboo material.

Though the character's Ottoman-Turkish name is Nasreddin Hoca, cognates such as Mullah or Sheikh Nasruddin, Djuha, Joha, Hodja, Abu Nuwas, and so on populate the folklore of Asian, African, European, and other cultures worldwide and share their narratives, so diverse cultural sources contribute to this collection.

The most readily accessible bawdy Nasreddin stories employ scatological, ethnic, racial, and sexist humor. Tales involving Nasreddin's wife Fatima and their extra-marital affairs are most prevalent, and many feature her as the sexual aggressor. The "young Nasruddin" tales often portray his pubescent sexual explorations and cunning sexual exploitation of women. Sexual stories involving Nasreddin's donkey make up a third recurring theme. Oddly, storylines with overtly homosexual themes were most difficult to unearth: even putting out a call for such jokes among today's Istanbul's gay and bisexual men's "bear" community yielded no results.

Other critical essays affirmed that these stories existed, although apparently not in contemporary English texts. Turkish scholar Seyfi Karabas observed that "erotic elements in Nasreddin Hoca narratives fulfill several important functions. To begin with, they point to various early stages in the development of Nasreddin Hoca as a trickster figure. Secondly, they serve to create humor in several ways." It was clear that examples of racy tales existed in the Nasreddin folklore corpus: the question was: *where?*

The lucky break in my research occurred in 2014 with a fortunate connection to Nasreddin Hoca and Turkish Studies scholar Hakkı Gűrkaş of Kennesaw College in Georgia, U.S.A., who provided me with several manuscripts containing many of the bawdy and taboo stories presented here.

In his brilliant, wide-ranging dissertation, Profesor Gűrkaş refutes the characterization of Nasreddin as a trickster figure, namely because of the lack of any sort of shape-shifting powers ascribed to him.

Regardless, Karabas sagely concludes that "awareness of the importance of sexuality in the life of human beings is one of the more persistent themes that help unify the whole corpus of the Nasreddin Hoca narratives. Hence, Nasreddin Hoca should not be laundered."

It appears that changing social forces of eight hundred years have taken Nasreddin Hoca's dirty laundry to the river and thrown it religiously against the rocks. This character purification began with linguistic and cultural changes brought in the transition from the Islamic Ottoman era to modern secular Turkish nationalism and continued through the advent of printing and selective exclusion of objectionable material from published story collections. Over the centuries, Nasreddin Hoca "transformed into a charming and subtle philosopher," according to Marzolph, "whose major preoccupation would be to confront his surroundings with apparently strange questions or unconventional solutions to common problems."

Gűrkaş explicates the social and literary significance of the censored material: "These stories bring back into discourse what the official culture has marginalized and repressed. These stories are anti-hegemonic. The grotesque imagery deployed in these stories mocks and ridicules the absolutist morality and degrades the official culture that relies on it."

Humorist and philosopher Jim Holt underscores the necessity of reclaiming this lost material: "If the history of folklore aspires to be a history of the human mind, . . . someone has to do the tedious job of collecting and recording obscene, disgusting, and blasphemous jokes, and ushering them into print."

In that spirit of intellectual freedom and restoration of the adulterated folklore, presented here are 257 authentic Nasreddin Hoca stories, many of which appear here in an English trade publication for the first time.

From the first volume, I rewrote more than a dozen stories, according to verified alternate sources: for instance, the long tale "Four brays of the donkey" here is "Four farts"; this version of "God's arrears to Nasruddin" has a Jewish protagonist; the sexual overtones in "Hens in the hammam" here are stated more fully.

Some stories are not particularly naughty, but come from reliable sources newly available and are worth including here among the first and final sections of the Mullah's adventures.

It is worthwhile repeating here that without exception, all narratives herein are based on published texts listed in the Sources; none of the tales presented in this or the first collection are my original or creative invention. I have retained a somewhat spare storytelling style considered a hallmark of multicultural folklore compilations.

Whenever multiple tellings of a joke or anecdote were available, the salient variations were incorporated into this work. However, for some stories, I had to rely on a computer translation of merely one or two versions and my ability to interpret its cultural context and narrative arc.

Also consistent with the previous collection, here I have employed the literary device of naming the Mullah's family, friends, neighbors, and donkey as a way to situate him in his community. I have tried to convey the bawdy wit and folk wisdom of the Mullah as may have been presented and received, centuries ago, halfway around the world, across three continents, by the original storytellers and listeners.

Granted, some readers will take offense at the intensity and frequency of the colloquial profanity and slang invective in parts of the narration and dialogue. The foul language, however, is comparable to that used in the stories listed in the Sources, albeit adapted to contemporary usage.

Folklore story collections like this are oddly situated between library and bookstore classifications of fiction and nonfiction. All the stories are made up by someone (fiction) — and yet folklore, like mythology, is classified as nonfiction by librarians and booksellers.

Since the stories are arranged among seven themed sections in a semi-random order, I recommend this book be read similarly, in a semi-random manner. This volume must be perused like a joke collection, not like a novel. Open the book to any page, read seven stories, and laugh, ponder, grimace, whatever — then save the rest for another time.

As exhaustive as this work may have been, this sequel and its predecessor do not represent the entire Nasreddin corpus. There are dozens of stories untranslatable from Turkish, German, Arabic, Persian, and other languages that remain inaccessible in English. Additionally, a handful of stories effectively translated, but requiring overlong cultural, religious, or wordplay explanations, must be left for another folklorist's work.

This compendium leads with "The learned and the ignorant," a tale that proclaims its moral imperative, "Those who know should teach those who don't know," which represents a common creed of folklore and literature. In researching, collecting, translating, retelling, and publishing these stories, I have acquired not only the authority to disseminate the work but also a keen sense of duty. For far too long, the social forces that repress sexual and other "undesirable" story elements have hidden this cache of some of the most amusing, witty, and outrageous folklore in the world.

I close this preface with the words of the great American poet, Walt Whitman: "The dirtiest book of all is the expurgated book." Doubtless, the Mullah would agree.

WORKS CITED

Gűrkaş, Hakkı. *Nasreddin Hodja and the Akşehir Festival: Invention of a Festive Tradition and Transfigurations of a Trickster, from Bukhara to Brussels.* Ph.D. dissertation. West Lafayette, Ind.: Purdue University, 2008.

Holt, Jim. *Stop Me if You've Heard This: A history and philosophy of jokes.* New York: W. W. Norton & Co., 2008.

Karabas, Seyfi. "The Use of Eroticism in Nasreddin Hoca Anecdotes." In *Western Folklore* 49: 3 (July 1990), pp. 299 – 305. Long Beach, Calif.: Western States Folklore Society.

Legman, Gershon. *The Horn Book: Studies in Erotic Folklore and Bibliography.* New Hyde Park, N.Y.: University Books, 1964.

Marzolph, Ulrich. *What Is Folklore Good For? On dealing with undesirable cultural expression.* In *Journal of Folklore Research*, 35: 1 (Jan. – Apr. 1998), pp. 5 – 16.

Traubel, Horace. *With Walt Whitman in Camden* (March 28 – July 14, 1888), by Journal Date: May 9, 1888, Quote Page 124. Boston: Small, Maynard & Co., 1906.

Extraordinary Adventures

OF
Mullah Nasruddin

Naughty, unexpurgated stories
of the beloved wise fool
from the Middle & Far East

REVISED EDITION

PART I

Mullah's Amazing Adventures

THE LEARNED AND THE IGNORANT

Centuries ago, in what is now central Turkey, in the rural town called Akşehir, Mullah Nasruddin was a respected tribal elder, spiritual guide, and judge. As such, on Fridays, the Mullah was expected to give the sermon for the Muslim Sabbath. Every week he would climb the steps to the pulpit in his mosque and hold forth on any number of topics before the congregation.

One particular Friday morning, however, even as he walked to the pulpit, nothing at all came to mind. Once upon the rostrum, as he stood before the assembled community, surveying the faces turned up toward him, finally an idea surfaced. Squaring his shoulders, Nasruddin announced in a powerful voice, "Oh true believers! Oh Muslims! Do you know the topic about which I have come to speak to you?"

Puzzled glances were exchanged, and then the people answered in hushed confusion, "No, we don't understand, not at all, we haven't a clue."

Nasruddin scowled at the congregation. "If you have no idea of the moral context and no clue as to the value of the message you are about to receive, then what can anything I tell you be worth?" And with that, he descended from the pulpit and exited the mosque, free for the time being. Of course, the entire next week, Nasruddin's cryptic sermon was the talk of the village.

That Friday, again Nasruddin found himself about to address the expectant flock with nothing to say. Taking the pulpit, he pointed from one side of the mosque to the other, and announced in an even more fiery tone, "Oh Muslims! Oh true believers! Do you have any idea of what I have come here to speak about?"

This time, the group, briefly looking around to confirm their mutual intention, rose and responded as one person, "Yes, we do know."

Nasruddin replied, "Oh, so now you all know everything there is to know about the subject, do you? If it's so obvious, then why should I waste my breath explaining to you what you already understand?" And he descended the pulpit stairs, reprieved for another week, while every man, woman, child, and donkey in town was all abuzz in anticipation of the next sermon from the inscrutable Mullah Nasruddin.

When, as it inevitably does, Friday came around once again, the Mullah found himself approaching the steps to the rostrum without a thought in his head. He slowly ascended the pulpit, then stood, silent, still and solemn, for an entire minute.

Then, shaking his fist, Nasruddin proclaimed in a furious roar that made every person in the mosque tremble with the fear of Allah, "Oh Muslims, oh true believers! Do you comprehend the topic about which I have come to speak to you today?"

As the group had agreed beforehand, half of the congregation stood up and said, "Yes, we know," while the other half remained seated and said, "No, we don't."

Every head in the room, whether seated or standing, craned forward to hear what the great Mullah Nasruddin had to say. "The people who do know — and you know who you are! — should teach those who don't know."

With his sermon concluded, the Mullah climbed down the pulpit. Looking neither left nor right, neither up nor down, neither inward nor outward, he scuttled out of the mosque, free and clear — at least, until the next Friday.

TWO SIDES OF A RIVER

One afternoon, Mullah Nasruddin was sitting peaceably on a bank along the Akşehir River, contemplating the infinite glory of God's creation.

A traveling stranger approached the stream from the opposite bank. After looking around a bit, the fellow noticed Nasruddin. He waved his arms and shouted, "Hey there, Mullah! Excuse me — please tell me, how do I get across the river?"

Without looking up, Nasruddin shouted back, "You *are* across!"

MOUTH WIDE SHUT

During a village meeting, a speaker talked uninterrupted for several hours, not letting anyone else get a word in edgewise. Nasruddin, sitting in the corner listening, yawned continuously throughout the fellow's endless pontifications.

When the fellow finally finished at the close of the meeting, the host turned to Nasruddin and said, "Well, folks, isn't that a shame! We did not have the pleasure of hearing our dear Mullah talk tonight. You haven't opened your mouth once."

"Are you kidding me?" cried the Mullah. "On the contrary, my poor jaw is now almost broken! It has come nearly unhinged from yawning so much."

SHEEP OF THE SEA

O nce, Mullah Nasruddin was traveling and arrived in the village square of a strange town. Before he knew it, he was drawn into a nasty argument with the pompous, implacable village mayor.

The mayor yelled at Nasruddin, "You insolent, rascally fool! Just as soon as the police come, I will have them throw you into a sack, tie it with a dozen ropes, and fling you into the sea!"

Nasruddin escaped and fled the village. On a meadow path, he met a well-built young shepherd tending a lovely flock, who said to him, "Where are you running, good Mullah, looking like a frightened rabbit?"

"I'm running to evade a most horrible fate!" answered the Mullah. "How can I not run? *Effendi*, I have taken a vow never to marry. But today, the Sultan has issued a proclamation that I should wed his beautiful daughter, and I will not ever!"

The shepherd said, "Are you out of your mind, Mullah? If I had that sort of luck, I would not be standing there with empty hands!"

Nasruddin replied, "Don't squander your youth tending sheep, my son. Your good fortune is to my benefit. If you are willing, you may put on my clothes, and I will wear yours. Thus, both of us will have our desires fulfilled."

The shepherd hardly could have expected this providential turn of events, and the two men quickly exchanged clothes. In his new shepherd's garb, Nasruddin drove the sheep away and retreated to a distance nearby to observe.

From his vantage point, he saw that the constables who tracked him down did not spend a long time figuring out whether he was Nasruddin or not. Seeing the man in the Mullah's clothes, they quickly slipped the bag over the shepherd's head, tied it fast, and threw him into the sea.

After Nasruddin saved himself from peril, he gathered his flock together and returned triumphantly home. When he arrived at the village center and drove so many beautiful sheep through the square, old and young alike wanted to witness the survival of Mullah, whom everyone knew the mayor made the police toss into the sea. They remarked to him, "By your faith you are alive, Mullah! Your survival is miraculous! How did you escape from the bag in the sea, and where did you acquire such a nice flock of cattle?"

"Funny thing, how that all happened," Nasruddin laughed. "When I was thrown into the sea, I struggled to tear myself out of the sack and swim back. As I was returning, I came upon a beautiful meadow, full of all sorts of sheep. What else could I do? I chose only the best animals, one by one, until I obtained enough, and continued on my way. I drove the cattle onto dry land, and now I am rich, Allah be praised! But I had to leave behind thousands more of these animals."

When the news got around town that there were so many free sheep in the sea, the poor gathered to enter the sea together and bring back the sheep. They tied a bag over each other's head and threw themselves into the sea. When the folks on the beach realized that no one returned from the sea, they asked Nasruddin, "Mullah, why haven't any of the others returned with so much cattle?"

He replied, "They certainly must have become greedy and lazy. Now that they have arrived at the place where they can take as much as they desire, they want so many of the sheep that they cannot drive them all. And surely they see that it is beautiful inside the sea, so they must have decided to stay there."

ONE LESS COIN TO PAY

Nasruddin was working as a ferryman when five blind men came and requested to be taken across the river. They negotiated a price of five silver pieces for all the men and their luggage.

Nasruddin helped the men board, then the dinghy left the dock in choppy waters. Nasruddin was such a clumsy oarsman that as he was trying to control the rocking boat, he knocked one of the blind men overboard. One of the other passengers said, "What happened? I thought I heard a splash."

Nasruddin said, "I have exceedingly good news for you. Once we arrive, you will have one silver piece less to pay for your fare."

TURBAN IS NO STRAP

Mullah Nasruddin was plowing his field when the well-worn leather strap he used to tie the ox to the yoke broke. There was no way the animal could pull the plow like this, so he unwrapped the turban from his head and used that to hold the yoke, but soon enough that failed as well.

He pointed at his now dirty, mangled turban, and addressed it, yelling, "All this time you've been so comfortable and lazy, just sitting atop my head all day long. I'll bet you never realized how hard the strap works, plowing the field, day after day. Now you get a taste of just how crappy it feels for the strap!"

GOD THREW HIS SHOE

One day in the chai shop, Mullah Nasruddin encountered an Armenian mendicant, who always carried the Bible around with him and read it ardently. The Mullah asked, "Tell me, sir, is the name of Muhammad mentioned in the Bible?"

"Yes, the name of Muhammad is there, at the very end," said the mendicant, delighted that this Mullah would take an interest in his Bible.

"So then please, read it to me!"

"Fine, it would be my pleasure." So the Armenian read aloud the last page of the Bible: " 'And thus it happened that while God was sitting with Mohammed on His right side, and Jesus Christ on His left. One day the Devil came and taunted God. God became angry and threw His sandal at the Devil. It hit the Devil, who ran away, but God's shoe fell into Hell. God asked Jesus to travel to the Underworld to retrieve His shoe. But Jesus refused to obey God and go.' "

At this, Nasruddin laughed, "Ha ha! God told Jesus to go to Hell to get His shoe, and Jesus snubbed Him!"

"Please allow me to continue," said the Armenian. " 'So God asked Muhammed, who agreed to journey down to Hell to get the shoe. But once Muhammad had arrived in Hell, the Devil closed the door behind Muhammad and locked it.' "

Nasruddin asked, "Then what happened?"

The Armenian turned the last page: there was nothing more. Nasruddin exclaimed, "So, according to your Bible, Mohammed was stuck in Hell!"

PENITENCE

Nasruddin was a homely fellow with unattractive features, although his long scraggly beard covered up a fair amount of his face. Once when he was in the market, a woman walked right up and stared at him with a cold, mean expression.

Nasruddin tried to ignore the woman, but when after several minutes she had not stopped gawking at him, he confronted her, "What does this mean — that you fix your sight on me with such a severe look on your face?"

The woman answered, "I have committed a great sin with my eyes and wanted to repent, so I vowed that I had to look at something completely repulsive to atone. I've been searching for days, and I could not find anything more unpleasant to look at than you."

WHITE DOG, BLACK DOG

Nasruddin's beard was already gray when, while walking along the road, he encountered a group of women leading a bride to her bridegroom. The Mullah lost his temper and called them obscene words.

They said, "Are you not at all ashamed? Doesn't a man with such a grizzled beard like yours know no restraint?"

The Mullah replied, "Does a white dog eat less shit than a black dog?"

PERSPECTIVE AND PERCEPTION

One day in the madrasa, Mullah Nasruddin was quizzing his students about various problems. He took out a quill pen and bottle of ink and began with deep concentration to draw something on a piece of paper.

When he finished drawing and the ink was dry, he handed the paper around to his students and asked, "Can any of you tell me what this is?"

The Mullah's students were flummoxed at their teacher's weird drawing. Some tried to give a religious answer, some offered a logical response, but to each of them the Mullah said only, "Incorrect," and shook his head.

Finally, when nobody would venture another guess, Nasruddin said, "You ignoramuses! Haven't you ever seen an ox pissing while it was walking?"

CURDS AND CRUMBS

Early one evening, a Kurdish fellow came to Mullah Nasruddin's house and asked for hospitality, saying, "My host, I've traveled for many weeks, and I'm exhausted and hungry! Please — let me take some rest in your house, and then I beg of you to give me something to eat."

The Mullah went to the kitchen, prepared an earthen bowl of yogurt, took some bread, and brought it all to the poor man. Then he saw the traveler had lain down and fallen deep asleep. So the Mullah wondered, "How can I convince him that he ate in his sleep?" Immediately he spread some yogurt on the bread and used that to smear the curds in the Kurd's mustache.

A few hours later, the Kurd awoke and cried, "Now please, kind sir, bring me something to eat!"

Then the Mullah replied, "But *effendi,* you've already eaten while you were asleep! If you do not believe my words, then look at your beard and mustache. They are still full of the curds and bread crumbs you devoured."

The Kurd put his hand to his beard and realized that his hair was full of curds and crumbs. Then the Kurd cried in scorn, "Very well, my host. If I have eaten and drunk, then God be praised!"

WHOSE PILE IS IT?

One day in Akşehir village, Nasruddin's neighbors, Hussein and Aslan, were chatting amiably in front of their houses when a stray dog came and shat right in the middle of the path, halfway between the houses.

Hussein asserted, "No doubt, that crap is nearer to your house. You should clean it up immediately."

Aslan protested, "Bullshit. It's closer to you. You must pick up the turds."

As the two argued, it became clear that neither would relent and so they decided to take their case to the local civil court.

As it so happened, that day the Mullah was in court serving as an assistant to the summary judge, when the two neighbors appeared in court to settle the dispute. The judge resented Nasruddin's claim to be an impartial arbitrator of common law. Secretly he wanted to flummox the famous Mullah and take him down a notch or two. He hoped that Nasruddin would be so confounded by the matter that the Mullah might end up having to pick up the dog crap himself.

The judge turned to Nasruddin and said, "Esteemed Mullah, in your great uncommon wisdom, you can arbitrate the matter before the court. Knowing this case is difficult, I will stand by your decision in this matter."

Nasruddin sat in the chair next to the judge and stroked his white beard. Then he stood again and asked the plaintiffs, "Tell the court in all honesty — is the pathway between your houses a public road?" Both men replied yes.

Nasruddin grabbed the judge's gavel and waved it around his head. "Then it is clear that neither party is obliged to clean up the crap. It is my decision, then, that, since this court's responsibility is to clear up civil matters in dispute, the responsibility for cleaning up the civic path is evenly split. Exactly one half of the crap belongs to you two, and the other half goes to . . . the civil judge."

EXTRACTION AND EXTRAPOLATION

Aslan came to Nasruddin, complaining, "I have a pain in my right eye. What advice do you have for me?"

"Just pull the bad eye out," said Nasruddin.

"Whatever gives you the idea that would work?" asked Aslan, horrified. "I've never heard of a remedy such as pulling out an eye."

"Don't you know anything? All last week I was plagued by a horrible toothache, which would simply not go away until I yanked it out. So if it worked for my tooth, it ought to work for your faulty eye."

BLACK SWEAT

Among Nasruddin's students was a dark-skinned Ethiopian lad named Hammad. One day just before class was to begin, the Mullah accidentally doused himself with black ink, and in his fumbling managed to blacken his hands and most of his face, head, and beard.

When his students walked into the room, they asked, "Mullah, what happened?"

He replied, "Hammad was late to class. To arrive in time, he ran so fast that he was sweating heavily when he came into the madrasa and embraced me. This blackness upon me must be his sweat."

THE PROPHET'S NEPHEW

As Mullah Nasruddin was leaving his home one morning, he saw a boy squatting in front of the entrance to the house, preparing to take a dump.

The Mullah shouted at the boy, "What do you think you are doing, you little dog? Whose son are you, whose accursed tribe I have fucked?"

The boy replied, "I am the nephew of the Prophet."

"Is that so?" Nasruddin yelled as he grabbed the boy by the hand and pulled his pants up. He dragged him away from the house and led him wordlessly to the mosque entrance. Then he pulled the boy's pants down and told him, "This is your uncle's house. Crap here all you like."

JEWISH WISDOM

While on the road, the Mullah met a learned rabbi named Yitzhak whose intellect impressed him. He asked the scholar, "Sir, is it possible for your most learned self to teach me Jewish wisdom?"

Rabbi Yitzhak replied, "Oh sure, it's possible, but it's by no means easy for a man of your meager means and puny build. It requires much will and effort, and you must possess both strength and endurance. The intricacies of Jewish mysticism cannot be taught or learned in one day, or a month, not really even in a year or more!" Nasruddin could not disguise his disappointment.

The Jew stroked his long black beard. "However, you seem like an earnest student, so I will attempt to impart Jewish wisdom to you in one intensive overnight lesson. Of course, for my extraordinary effort and exemplary wisdom, you're going to have to pay me a lot of money!"

"I only have a few coins right now to offer you. Once I've attained something, I can afford your full fee," said the Mullah.

The rabbi agreed, "Fine. But before we begin your lesson, you ought to bathe well and wear clean clothes. Come at dawn so we can start working early."

The Mullah rested, washed up, and dressed appropriately. Then he returned to Rabbi Yitzhak, who instructed, "The first element in learning Jewish mysticism is trust. Though daylight is coming, you must learn to see without using your eyes. Prepare to use your other senses to guide you."

He blindfolded the Mullah and led him out of the village and into the woods. When they had gone far enough, the rabbi said, "All right, to begin your teaching, I'll have to tie you up." He tied Mullah fast to a sturdy cypress tree and said, "I must relieve myself, then I'll be back. You are to remain here for my return, and then the first lesson will begin."

Even though he was not in any position to do otherwise, Mullah waited silently, an hour, two hours, all day. The sun went down, and he was cold. The sun came up. Still, he awaited the arrival of his Jewish wisdom.

Finally that morning, a burly hunter tracking game in the woods happened to see the Mullah in his predicament. He cut the blindfold and released him from the tree, asking, "What happened to you, poor Mullah? Were you robbed? What are you doing here?"

"Leave me alone, you jackass. Just go away before you fuck it all up!" yelled the Mullah, still clinging to his tree.

"You're daft, man," laughed the hunter. "You would have died if I hadn't come by and set you free. Why do you want to send me away?"

"Devil take you! You're interrupting my training! You're going to ruin everything. Can't you see that I'm an ardent student just trying to gain Jewish insight?"

"No doubt you're here to learn Jewish wisdom," replied the hunter, laughing even harder. "And I admit, this is certainly a fine example of their craftiness. But I hate to inform you — you're the victim here."

HOW THE WATER COMES TO THE MILL

Once young Nasruddin came upon a windmill. He had never seen anything like it before, so he went to the miller and asked him, "Please, kind sir, tell me — what is that thing called?"

The man replied, "This is called a windmill, son."

"And please tell me, where does the water come from, to operate this mill?" asked the boy.

The miller answered, "This is a windmill — no water is involved."

"Sure, you're right. I get that," replied Nasruddin. "But nevertheless, how does the water come to this mill?"

Centuries ago in the days of windmills and waterwheels, this story's punch line — *How does the water come to the mill?* — became a popular saying. The axiom represents an apparent contradiction when two or more distinct operations or functions are conflated by mistake.

ACCUMULATED MERIT

Nasruddin heard an imam declare in the mosque one day that anyone who fasts on the Muslim holy day of Ashura will undoubtedly attain the full equivalent religious benefit of fasting for a whole year.

When the holiday came, the Mullah devoutly fasted until midday, then broke the fast by eating a large and sumptuous lunch at home.

When Fatima discovered her husband rubbing his stomach and burping, she asked what he was doing. He simply replied, "I've already earned enough merit from observing Lent all this morning to last me through the rest of the year."

FRUITS OF LABOR

Mullah Nasruddin went into the hills one day to chop timber and brought some fresh melons to eat. By the time he arrived at the woods, he was quite thirsty, so he sliced open one of the fruits and took a bite, but found it not sweet enough and threw it away. Then he cut another piece of melon, sampled it, and tossed that slice on the other one.

Before long, he had cut up all of the melons, tasted just a tiny bit of each slice, and found none of them worth eating. His frustration turned to anger, and he pissed on the pile of discarded fruit. Then he went to work and felled wood.

After several hours, when Nasruddin had chopped enough firewood for the day, he took a break before loading it all onto his little gray donkey, and heading home. He was parched, but couldn't find any water nearby.

He picked up one of the discarded melon slices, examined it, and said, "This slice has gotten only a little dirty," and ate it. Then he chose another and said, "This piece is also perfectly edible," and ate that. Then he reasoned, "The rest of these are probably not so bad, either."

At last, there remained only a heap of melon peels. "Good thing," Nasruddin thought, as he began to load the firewood on his little donkey's back before heading home, "that I didn't crap on that fruit."

A STUPID BEARD

Nasruddin was listening to a sermon in the mosque one day when the imam declared angrily, "Anyone who wears a beard longer than his fist is stupid."

When the Mullah returned home, he checked himself in the mirror and realized that his beard was quite a bit longer than his fist. He lit a candle, intending to burn off only an inch or so of the offending hairs — just the part that was hanging below his fist.

Whoosh! In a flash, his beard went up in flames, and he could not put it out before singeing his skin. Now Nasruddin's face looked like a half-plucked chicken.

The next day, Nasruddin went to see the imam, and said, "What you told me yesterday about the proper beard length was completely correct. A man with a long beard possesses short wisdom. It's true that I lost my beard and burned my face, but at least now, I am free of being stupid."

HIS SINS ARE REVEALED

Once, Nasruddin went on *hajj*, the long pilgrimage to Mecca. Throngs of pious pilgrims from all over the world crowded to enter the *Kaaba*, which is the sanctum sanctorum of all Muslims. As he reached the threshold, many people, including a black Ethiopian man, were pressed together.

One of the privileged visitors protested, crying, "Oh Lord! How can You admit to this holiest of holy sites, this black savage unbeliever?"

Nasruddin saw this and told the whining man, "Oh, shut up, you hypocritical sinner! Why do you insult this man here because of the dark color of his flesh? At least he is open to showing his transgressions outwardly on his skin. If we had the honesty and courage to reveal our many sins before everyone, then you and I would probably appear blacker than him."

COMMANDER OF THE RATS

Mullah Nasruddin once collaborated with his Jewish neighbor, Aslan, to trade in metal. They agreed to stockpile a quantity of cheap iron for several years and sell it when the price increased. So Nasruddin and Aslan proceeded to buy large amounts of the metal, which they stored on the ground floor of the Jew's home.

Secretly Aslan sold the iron little by little without Nasruddin learning about it. Eventually, when finally the prices were advantageous, Mullah told Aslan, "We should sell our iron now that it is trading high."

"Terribly sorry, chum, but I have discovered that the rats have eaten it," replied his partner. "Just this morning when I went down to the storeroom to check the iron, I realized I had a rodent infestation. I searched throughout the cellar, in every corner, and all I found were black rat turds. Those horrible rats must have eaten our iron."

"Impossible!" Mullah fumed. "Rats do not eat iron. If that's how you're going to behave, then I'll bring you before the judge."

"Fine, as you wish," said Aslan. "But now it is evening. We can go to the magistrate early tomorrow morning."

Straightway after the Mullah left, Aslan went to the judge's house, where he told the judge the story of the disappearing iron and offered him a bribe. As the judge pocketed the money, he said, "No problem, come back tomorrow with that fool Nasruddin. We'll settle it quickly and be done with him."

The next morning Mullah and Aslan appeared before the judge, and each man described their version of the situation. The judge stroked his beard and said to the Mullah, "Well, my friend, it's true that rats eat iron. I remember when I was very young, my mother once put some tallow in a copper mortar. The rats had bit holes in the mortar and ate the tallow. Go away now, Nasruddin. You sued your partner for nothing."

Nasruddin left the local court and went directly to the Sultan. "I have come here to beg you a small favor," Nasruddin said. "I wish to be appointed 'Commander of the Rats' and given full authority with written proof." The Sultan knew that the Mullah was up to something, but he couldn't think of a reasonable excuse to deny the request, so he issued a proclamation stating that the Mullah was hereby commissioned as a commanding officer of all the rats in their region, and Nasruddin took the decree.

Armed with this signed and sealed document, Mullah went to the village square where day-laborers were gathered in search of work. There he saw a group of scruffy but well-built young men standing with their sledgehammers, picks, and shovels. He approached the group, saying, "Hey, you donkeyfuckers — come work for me. I'll give you two gold coins every day."

He selected five of the beefiest, toughest-looking men of the group and led them to the Jew's house. There he ordered the men to strip off their shirts and destroy the foundation of the house.

Aslan, who had been sitting quietly at home, was stupefied at the pounding at the outside walls and swaying of his house. He looked out his window and saw Mullah directing his band of half-naked musclemen as they spared no sweat in attacking the foundation. He yelled at Nasruddin, "Stop it, you asshole! What is the meaning of this? Make them stop at once!"

Nasruddin shouted for his crew to halt the wrecking. Then he raised above his head the Sultan's proclamation and announced, "By virtue of my duly appointed office as Commander of the Rats, I am authorized to search for, arrest, and take into custody the rats that ate my iron on these premises."

When Aslan got downstairs, he screamed, "Are you fucking crazy, Nasruddin? What office do you hold that gives you the right to attack my house?"

"Look here," said Mullah, holding up his commission from the Sultan.

When Aslan got downstairs and read the decree, he screamed, "What is this crap? It says here that you are the Commander of the Rats!"

"As I already informed you," Nasruddin said. "I assure you, we will find those scoundrels wherever they have hidden. They will be given a fair trial — perhaps by your good friend, the judge, who also knows rats so well — and, if necessary, we will punish them. Thus justice will be served."

"Hold on, Nasruddin!" cried Aslan. "I'll give you the money for your iron and again as much. But halt your search for the rats who ate the missing metal!"

Mullah paid his demolition crew and pocketed the rest of the money.

They proceeded to the judge's front door, where Nasruddin knocked. As the judge opened the door and stepped outside, the Mullah commanded the brawny bunch, "Demolish the foundation!"

"Wait, wait! What in Allah's name is going on?" roared the judge.

"I have a decree from the Sultan declaring that I am the Commander of the Rats," stated Nasruddin. "I am here as a favor to you, to avenge the wrongdoing of your childhood that you described to me."

"What are you talking about, Nasruddin?"

"As I am now duly authorized to arrest and prosecute all the rats in the region, I have come to your house as the first stop on a search mission. I'm looking for all the rats that have perforated a copper mortar to eat the tallow, to bring them at long last to justice."

The judge was astonished by the Mullah's cunning and awarded him an even more enormous sum than the fee paid by the Jew.

A FINE HAIRCUT

One day, Nasruddin entered a barbershop followed by a young boy. He told the barber that he was in a hurry and wanted to get his hair cut first. The barber readily agreed and proceeded to give Nasruddin a proper hair styling. Naturally, since the Mullah was nearly bald, this consisted mostly of trimming his beard. Nasruddin checked his hair, replaced his turban, told the boy and the barber he'd be back soon, and left.

The boy hopped into the barber chair, and the barber trimmed his hair. After this haircut was done, the boy got out of the chair and started to leave. The barber stopped him and said, "But where is your father? He said he'd be right back, and now he's late."

"Father?" the boy replied. "That man isn't my father. He's just some guy I met on the street outside who told me to come in for a free haircut."

INDIGESTIBLE MATTERS

I n the chai shop one day, Aslan queried Nasruddin, "Whatever I eat, it seems, I can never digest it properly. Kindly give me your opinion: what should I do?"

Mullah advised, "This is not difficult: Simply eat only what others have already digested."

HEAVENLY SPHERES

T he great mystic, Scheyyad Hamza, once met the famous Mullah Nasruddin and said, "So Mullah, what's up with you? Is it true that your only work in the world is to tell jokes and act absurdly? If you have any other talent, please inform me of it, for I would like to know what it is."

Nasruddin replied, "Yes. One talent is enough. And what have you got to show as your contribution to the world, Mr. Perfection?"

Scheyyad Hamza said, "My skills and advantages are endless. Every night I leave the world of human beings and fly up to the limits of the first firmament to meet the angels. When I arrive at the bottom of the celestial realm, I reach upward into the sky to touch what can be found at its base."

Mullah asked, "Does your hand ever touch something as tender and soft as sable and lynx?"

Scheyyad Hamza replied, "No."

Mullah said, "Well, next time you go flying, what you see there and what your hand touches will be the hair of my balls: just grab them and hold on tight!"

A LADDER TO HEAVEN

O nce while traveling, Nasruddin engaged in a religious debate with a Greek Orthodox priest.

"Mullah," queried the priest, "how did your Prophet Mohammed ascend to Heaven, pray tell?"

Nasruddin simply responded, "With the ladder left behind by your prophets, my prophets actually climbed up and reached Heaven."

HOT COUTURE

One blazing hot afternoon at the chai shop, Mullah and the wags were discussing travels to distant lands. Faik declared, "I've heard of desert regions where it is so abominably hot, everyone just walks around completely naked all the time."

Nasruddin queried, "Without clothes, how in the world do they tell the women from the men?

WITH THE LUCK YOU BROUGHT

Hamid, a sadistic barber, returned to Akşehir from a weeklong vacation trip to a town he had never visited before. Nasruddin asked how his week went.

"Oh grand, I must say, everything was fine for my companions and me."

"That's good to hear. What did you do?"

"Oh, not much. But lucky for us, it seemed everywhere around us amusing and intriguing things were happening."

"Do tell," encouraged the Mullah.

"On Monday, a fire broke out at the edge of the village and razed about five homes, all in a row. We watched it all. There were a few lives lost, but all in all, it wasn't too bad. One fellow's mother-in-law perished, and he seemed quite bereft."

"Oh my," said the Mullah.

"Tuesday morning, a mad dog bit two men. They brought the men to me to treat them, and so I burned the flesh of the two so that they wouldn't go mad as well, and they bellowed like bison at the pain, but then they disposed of the dog in a most unfortunate way, and that seemed to make everyone feel better."

"You don't say."

"It's true. On Wednesday, there was a sudden toerrential downpour, and the town was flooded. Several houses were washed away. Many animals were also swept up in the strong current. But the most curious thing was the household furniture floating around — a cradle, for example, with an infant in it — all heading downriver. So that kept us amused until dinnertime."

"What happened the next day?"

"Well, on Thursday a crazed bull broke loose and terrorized the remaining citizens. It wounded four or five folks, put out one fellow's eye, and gored another man's intestines. It was unclear if the man would live."

"Did the disasters take a break for the Sabbath?" asked Nasruddin.

"Oh, not at all, the fun just never seemed to end. Friday morning, a deranged villager ran amok and mortally stabbed her husband and their two children. That made us very angry, and so we joined a mob who went to the woman's house and stoned the sorry soul to death."

"I hesitate to ask what happened on Saturday."

"Let me tell you. The next day, following an earthquake, the old tile roof over the market collapsed, crushing nearly everyone underneath. Men, women, and children were buried under the ruins, and their screams for mercy could be heard for miles.

"After a lovely lunch, I went down to the bazaar and tried to help clear away some of the rubbish. By then, as there was nothing of great value to be discovered and the wounded were quite horrible to view and smell, I thought it best not to linger, and so I guess they perished, screaming in pain until their last breaths.

"On Sunday, a woman who had lost her entire family in the earthquake the day before hanged herself on a willow tree behind what remained of her house. When we went to see that, we were told that she was the woman who had lost a nursing baby in a crib in the flood on Wednesday.

"By then, since the town was largely devastated and there was little else to keep us occupied, we decided to cut the trip short and come home."

Nasruddin said, "So, you had quite a week, it seems."

"As our good fortune would have it, yes, it was splendid. We were indeed lucky not to be bored in the least for even a day."

"Praise Allah, it's auspicious that you chose to return early!" exclaimed the Mullah.

"Why, Mullah — whatever do you mean?"

"With the luck you brought them, had you remained in their village any longer, there is no doubt that neither a creature would be left alive nor a single stone standing atop another."

MOTHER OF CUNNING

One day a group of women stood on the banks of the Akşehir River looking at the water. Mullah Nasruddin saw them and asked the apparent matriarch of the group, "Kind mother, tell me: what are you waiting here for?"

She replied, "We did not know how to get to the other side. If you carry us over, we'll each give you a dinar."

Immediately the Mullah took off his clothes, got into the water, and brought them over, one by one. Finally, only the old woman remained. As she had been watching the near-naked Nasruddin carrying her friends across the river, she was overcome by lust. He picked the woman up and waded into the water. She said, "I must confess, Mullah, I have fallen in love with you. Look here: do you not know who I am?"

"No idea. Who are you?" asked the Mullah.

She replied, "I am the mother of cunning."

"Even if you're the mother of faith," said the Mullah, "then it would not prevent me from taking you as a man."

He took her clothes off, put himself inside, and started to fuck her. While he was thrusting, suddenly he let out a fart.

The woman exclaimed, "Mullah, what are you doing?"

But he only replied, "Mother, the great pleasure that you have opened to me, has also opened me a bit."

A YEAR AND A DAY

Nasruddin's student Imad queried him, "Legend has it that the hawk lives six months as a male, then six months as a female. Mullah, is that true?"

"As for myself, I do not have the answer to your question," Nasruddin replied. "However, I can tell you this much: to know, you must find someone who has been a hawk for a year and a day."

RIGHT BEFORE HIS EYES

Mullah Nasruddin, who was visiting his friend Jalal in Konya for a few days, was chewing gum and chatting with his host when Jalal's wife invited him to join the family for dinner. So Nasruddin sat down at the table, took the wad of gum out of his mouth, and stuck it on his nose before he tucked in.

Jalal asked, "Mullah, can you please explain to me why you have placed your gum on your nose?"

Nasruddin replied, "Poor people always have to keep their property right before their eyes!"

PROXY PROTECTOR

M ullah Nasruddin was traveling one day with his old friend Hussein. When night fell, they stopped at a crossroads.

Hoping to spend the night alone with his donkey, Nasruddin told Hussein, "It's been delightful, but tonight I am planning to spend the night here under the starry sky. You need not stay with me if you want to continue to travel. Your town is not too far from here."

"What are you talking about, Nasruddin? It's still at least a half day's walk. I insist on keeping you company, and I assure you that I'd much prefer to sleep here as well, rather than walk home alone at night."

"Are you sure you're sure? Have you appointed someone to protect your wife's virtue in your absence?" Nasruddin asked.

"Yes, Mullah," said Hussein, "I asked my good friend and neighbor Hamza to guard my wife's virtue while I'm away."

"But whom, may I ask," inquired Nasruddin, "have you appointed to look after the virtue of your good friend and neighbor Hamza?"

DOUBLE THE DONKEYS

O ne day in the imperial court, the Sultan, pleased with Nasruddin's seemingly endless wit and wisdom, said to the Mullah, "Request of me anything that you will!"

Nasruddin replied, "Your Lordship, if it pleases you, I would ask only that you provide me with a document that stipulates this: from every man whom I can prove is afraid of his wife, I may take a donkey."

The Sultan said, "Consider it done!" Mullah received the decree, then traveled to villages in the environs of the city and, after a few days, he returned.

The Sultan was sitting at his palace window when he noticed a small cloud of dust on the horizon. A low rumbling grew steadily as it drew closer. Before long he could discern that Nasruddin was driving a thundering herd of donkeys toward the cattle market.

When he saw the Mullah that day in court, the Sultan exclaimed, "I am amazed to see the evidence that so many men fear their wives. Please tell me the true story of what happened."

Mullah said, "Indeed, your Majesty, this is the sad state of the males in your kingdom. Did you not give me the command to take one donkey from every man who fears his wife?" The Sultan nodded.

"Let me tell you: I traveled far and wide, but at every place I visited, I found that the men were cowed by their wives." At this, the Mullah gave the Sultan a roguish look, winked, and leaned forward to confide in him.

"By the way — I must mention this for I know of your keen interest in such things — while in one village, I saw a girl as beautiful as the moon, with cheeks like pomegranates, eyes like that of gazelles, and ample breasts of alabaster. Undoubtedly this girl is a virgin, but with a beguiling demeanor that would make you shudder until you fainted away with delight and joy."

The Sultan whispered, "Shhh, please, Mullah — quiet! My wife is sitting behind that screen. Speak a little quieter, or else she will overhear you!"

Mullah stroked his beard and declared, "Of all the other men, I've always only taken a single donkey. But from you, I want two — and make them white ones."

NASRUDDIN'S NAIL (DJUHA'S NAIL)

A neighbor of Nasruddin, Aslan, was a portly, hairy Jew with a thick, bushy mustache. For years since he had moved to their village, Aslan was keenly aware of the Mullah's ongoing financial difficulties and sought an opportunity to take maximum advantage of the situation.

One day Aslan paid a neighborly visit to the Mullah's modest house and looked around. "I would dearly like to help you, my dear friend. I will buy the house from you, even though it's dilapidated, and I don't really have any interest in spending much money for it." The man offered a pitiful price, half of the actual value of the property.

Nasruddin sighed and drew a small piece of paper from the folds of his clothing. "God bless you with long life and healthy progeny for this kind gesture, my neighbor! Indeed, for months, I have been praying for such a generous offer. The house indeed shall be yours, just as soon as we take care of this little clause in the contract."

"What clause?" asked Aslan, suspicious of his wily neighbor.

"It is only an insignificant matter — just a technicality. As you are aware, this house was built by my father, Yousef. I was born in this house."

"A fine gentleman he was," admitted Aslan. "Always paid in cash."

"And you see here on the wall of the living room — there is one nail sticking out. My father never had the chance to finish hammering it in. He had a heart attack and died."

"God rest his soul!" Aslan looked as contrite as he could.

"Therefore, I request that I be allowed to keep full ownership of that nail and to do whatever I want with it. The nail is off-limits to you and your wife, and you cannot otherwise interfere with my nail or its functioning."

Aslan reluctantly agreed but explained that he would have to consult his wife, Rabia, before he could sign the contract. When he told her about the deal, she raised some serious objections. "Why does that scallywag want to leave one old bent nail in the wall? What does it mean?"

"Who knows? Sentimental memories of his dad, maybe. He just wants to be allowed to keep and 'worship' that nail from time to time. That's all, pumpkin. What else could he want with it? Harmless, I'm sure."

"Well, I'm not so sure about that," she said. "We've known Nasruddin and his family for many years, and my conclusion is that that man is one whacked-out son of a bitch!"

"Maybe so. But the house is actually in decent shape, and we are getting it for less than half its value. So what's the problem if he wants to keep a single stupid nail? We can move in there and rent out this house."

Rabia finally relented, and the two men put in writing all the considerations of the sale of the property, including Nasruddin's requirement regarding his father's special nail, and signed the contract.

One week after Nasruddin had vacated the house, Aslan and Rabia were just sitting down for dinner when they heard a knock on the door. It was none other than Mullah Nasruddin, standing with his head bowed.

"Hello, Mullah, where have you been? We were worried about you," the Jew declared.

Nasruddin said, "Thank you for your concern, kind neighbor. I wish to worship my father's nail."

"Not a good time. We're just about to eat."

"Go ahead and eat. I just want to pay my respects silently and leave. I'll let myself out." Reluctantly Aslan let him into the house.

Mullah silently entered and walked up to his nail, prostrated, and put his scarf on it. Then he sat cross-legged on the floor with his eyes closed, becoming deeply absorbed in meditation. After ten minutes, Aslan came in to check on him just as the Mullah bowed again and stood up and headed for the door.

Aslan pointed to the nail and asked, "Hey Mullah, what in Allah's name is that thing doing there?"

"That's just my scarf."

"Yes, but you can't leave your crap in my house right here now."

"Of course I can leave it right here now, to retrieve it right here later," said the Mullah as he headed toward the door. "It's on my nail."

Three days passed before Nasruddin's next visit.

Aslan greeted him, saying, "Ah, good morning, Mullah. You have come to get your scarf, I presume."

"No, thank you, my dear friend. I have come today simply to worship my dear departed father's holy nail."

As before, Nasruddin bowed to the nail and meditated for ten minutes. His worship finished, he bowed again and stood up. Then he hung his turban along with the scarf on his nail and quickly left. Aslan slammed the door behind the departing Mullah and hoped his wife wouldn't notice, or if she did see it, that she wouldn't be too angry.

Indeed, Rabia immediately noticed the turban, and she was furious. "Enough is enough, you old fool. I told you he would try to pull a fast one on us."

"Sadly there is little or nothing that we can do about the matter," Aslan told her, knawing at the ends of his mustache. "Nasruddin claims he is worshipping his dead father's nail and we signed away the rights to that nail. Certainly, this must be the last time. If you don't look at it, it's out of your mind anyway, so just ignore it. Anyway, pumpkin, what else can he possibly hang on the nail?"

The very next day, when Nasruddin returned, Aslan objected to his visiting his father's nail so frequently. "We need to have a compromise on the times and frequency you can visit."

"You signed the contract. You know you cannot deny me the chance to pay tribute to the sole sacred memento of my dear departed father — whenever I like or in any manner I choose, without limitation."

Mullah stepped quickly into the house and bowed toward his nail, then sat, becoming absorbed in his meditation. After ten minutes, he bowed again toward the nail, stood up to leave, then took off his coat and hung it on the nail along with the turban and scarf.

After Nasruddin left, Rabia was beside herself with anger, and she upbraided her husband. "Now look what that weasel has done! He is taking advantage of our kindness. No — he is taking advantage of your weakness!

"What can I do?" Aslan chewed the ragged bristle of his mustache. "We agreed that he could do whatever he wants with his nail. But fear not, pumpkin, now the nail is completely full. There is absolutely nothing else he can do to annoy us."

The next day, Nasruddin showed up again. Aslan tried to shut the door in his face when he saw who it was, but the Mullah had already placed his foot inside. "Oh, dear God. Not you again. I do hope this is the last time!"

"In a world of infinite possibilities," replied Nasruddin with his usual benign smile, "that is certainly a possibility. But not likely."

"Nasruddin, you can't keep leaving things on the nail."

"Oh, yes I can, effendi. You should know by now that nothing is going to stop me from worshipping my father's memorial nail. But in fact, I was planning this visit that I'd take the things I left on the nail with me."

"Well, thank Allah for small favors," said Aslan, relieved as he opened the door. Mullah entered, carrying with one hand what appeared to be part of a dead goat. With the other hand, he took the hat, scarf, and coat off his nail. Then he proceeded to hang the goat carcass on it.

As the Mullah donned his cloak, scarf, and turban, Rabia went ballistic and screamed at her husband, "Get that dead goat out of my house or I'm leaving you!"

The Jew protested vehemently, "Nasruddin, now you've really gone too far. We cannot have that." Aslan bit at the stubble on his upper lip.

"But you signed the contract, good neighbor. And since you've already admitted and allowed these other objects to be hung on my nail, you cannot object to my leaving my meat to cure here."

"Well, we will see about that. Let us have the council of elders make a ruling."

"Fine. The elders meet in three days. We'll settle this once and for all by then. Meanwhile, keep your hands off my nail."

In two days, the stench and buzzing insects filled the interior of the house until it was a nightmare to stay anywhere inside. Since their old house was occupied, Rabia moved back to her parents.

The next day, before the assembly of village elders, Aslan explained the situation, anxiously picking at the few wisps remaining from his once bristling mustache, as though the sprouts of hair offended him.

Mullah simply presented the contract to the council, without uttering a word in his defense.

The village leaders studied the contract in a conference and quickly pronounced that the Mullah was entitled to do as he wished with his nail. "Clearly there are no limitations in the contract that restrict how the nail may be worshipped." The case was dismissed, and Aslan went home dejected.

The next morning, after a sleepless night, Aslan begged Mullah to buy back his house at a fraction of the sale price. Nasruddin agreed and the Jew moved out as quickly as possible.

Whistling a happy tune, Nasruddin returned home, opened all the doors and windows, cut down and disposed of the dead goat, cleaned the house, and moved back in. So the Mullah once again was able to enjoy his home and his father's nail, having made a tidy sum of money.

Since then, the term "Nasruddin's nail" (or "Djuha's nail") has become a proverbial phrase somewhat like what we nowadays call a "poison pill," a seemingly advantageous situation that has a small but severe or fatal drawback with the potential to spoil or sour the deal.

PART II

Young Nasruddin

LORD, LEAVE ME ALONE

Nasruddin's mother, Leyla, thought her young son was, at the bottom, a lost cause. She didn't know what to do with him, so as a last resort, she hired him as an errand boy to an innkeeper.

The innkeeper instructed him, "Okay kid, go to the shore and wash out this old wineskin. But do it properly; otherwise, you will receive a severe punishment!" So, rather than go to the nearby river, Nasruddin took the wineskin to the sea.

It took the boy a few hours to walk there, but he immediately set to his task. And there he washed the wineskin, filling and emptying it over and again, and continued cleaning it out through the long morning. By the time the sun shone directly above, he wondered, *How do I know if this dumb old wineskin is washed well enough? Who is nearby, whose opinion I can ask about this?*

There wasn't a single person on the beach, but offshore was anchored a deep-sea fishing ship, with several of its crew on deck. Nasruddin waved the wineskin as a signal, and shouted, "Ahoy! Can you help me? Sir, can you bring me there?"

The ship was preparing to pull up anchor and head out to sea when the captain noticed the boy yelling. "There, on the shore, is a child calling in distress," he said. "We must rescue him! You, sailor, row with a sloop to the shore and fetch the boy."

Finally, when Nasruddin stood before him, the Captain asked, "What is the matter, boy?"

"Please tell me, kind sir," Nasruddin enquired, "in your esteemed opinion, is this wineskin well washed?"

Although the captain was just one man, he had the strength of ten. He put the boy over his knee and spanked him until the boy was nearly senseless. Weeping in pain, Nasruddin cried out, "What was I supposed to say?"

"Idiot, you should have said instead: 'Lord, let them go! Lord, let them depart!' Now we must try to regain the time that we have lost because of you."

They took Nasruddin back and dumped him in the shallow water, at which point he threw the wineskin over his shoulder and left the shore. As he made his way across the fields, he chanted his new mantra: "Lord, let them go! Lord, let them get away!"

He came upon a hungry hunter who was about to shoot at two rabbits. Nasruddin shouted, "Lord, let them get away! Lord, let them flee!" The rabbits naturally jumped up and scampered away.

The hunter shouted, "Oh, you little bastard! I just missed getting a nice fat rabbit! You screwed up my hunt!" And he slapped the boy on his face five times.

Nasruddin asked, "What should I have said?"

"Isn't it obvious? What you should be praying is: 'Lord, let them be killed!' or "Lord, let them both die!' "

With the wineskin over his shoulder, Nasruddin headed onward, repeating, "Lord, let them be killed. Lord, let them both die."

And whom did the boy next meet on the road? Two big bearish brutes embroiled in a heated dispute that had come to blows. Nasruddin fearfully spoke, "Lord, let them both die. Lord, let them kill themselves."

When the two adversaries heard this, they stopped fighting each other and turned upon the boy, saying, "You puny punk! Want to stir up some trouble for yourself?" And in cordial harmony, they proceeded to smack him around.

When Nasruddin could speak, he cried out, "Please stop — that is not what I meant! But what should I have said?"

"What should you say? You should repeat: 'Lord, let them separate!' "

"Well, Lord, let them separate! Lord, let them part ways!" muttered Nasruddin to himself, as he left the men.

Before long, Nasruddin passed by a church where emerged a bride and groom who had just wed. As soon as the bride heard the boy intoning the words, "Lord, let them separate!" she made her new husband defend their sacred marriage. The man took off his belt and beat Nasruddin with it as he screamed, "You miserable devil! You want me to separate from my wife?"

Nasruddin, who could no longer defend himself, fell to the ground like a dead man. When the bride had raised him again, he opened his eyes, and she asked, "Why in the world would you have the lack of sense to say something like that to a new bride and groom?"

Nasruddin replied, "I have no idea why I say anything at all. So tell me, please: what words should I have used?"

"You ought to have said: 'Lord, let them laugh forever'!"

Nasruddin retrieved his wineskin and went off again, repeating the phrase over to himself, hoping he wouldn't fail again. Then he passed a house where a wake for a dead man was in progress, with relatives mourning, standing around holding candles. When the deceased person's family heard Nasruddin intoning, "Lord, let them laugh forever," they attacked him. And he received in full what yet he lacked in abuse.

After they finished with him, Nasruddin realized that it was better to keep his mouth shut — though he could barely move his split, bloody lips to speak anyway — and return to the inn.

When the innkeeper saw the boy return in the evening, having sent him early in the morning to wash the wineskin, he demanded, "Tell me, you worthless shithead, where were you all this time?"

But Nasruddin could not utter a single word in his defense. So the innkeeper gave the boy one more spanking and sent him home.

In a hurry

When Nasruddin was a child, like all young Turks his age, he attended the grade school for boys, the *madrasa*, in the village of Akşehir.

One morning, young Nasruddin ran stark naked through the town square and into the madrasa. As he raced by, his friend Hussein called out, "Nasruddin, why aren't you dressed properly?"

"I overslept for the big test today," said Nasruddin, trying to cover himself and jog in place to respond, "and so in my crazy rush to make it to school on time, I forgot to put on clothes."

Payback's a bitch

Once when young Nasruddin cursed at his mother, his father Yousef scolded him, "Damn you, demon child! I've had enough of your disrespect for your mother. What kind of way is that to thank her for everything she has given you?"

The boy retorted, "What has she ever done for me?"

Yousef said, "In case you forgot, you ungrateful moron, she bore you for nine months in her womb, and she has reared and nourished you all these years."

Nasruddin replied, "So tell her to crawl up my ass, then I will bear her for nineteen months for her sake, and we'll call it even."

IF YOUR DREAM IS TRUE

One night, young Nasruddin was sleeping with his mother, Leyla, in the same bed, when she let rip a loud fart.

Because Leyla was embarrassed by her trump, she said quickly, "My son! I dreamed of dark clouds, lightning, and a loud rumbling like a thunderstorm."

Nasruddin replied, "If your stinky dream proves to be true, soon it will be raining shit on us!"

WHOSE PLEASURE IS IT?

Nasruddin came to his mother one day and found her weeping. He asked her why, and she cried, "Your father promised to sleep with me, but then he suddenly walked away."

Nasruddin asked where his father was, and she told him that he was in the mosque. He went there and found his father inside just as the leader had ended the prayer, but the congregation had not yet left.

Nasruddin called out to the prayer leader, "Sir! Wait!" Then he asked his father, "Why aren't you sleeping with my mother?"

Yousef replied, "She no longer pleases me."

But Nasruddin contradicted him, "I swear to God, even if a hundred men lined up to screw my mother, she would satisfy all of them!"

The people laughed at this, and Nasruddin's father was ashamed.

MISTAKEN IDENTITY

Yousef, Nasruddin's father, was in the toilet with the door closed and window open, and let out a loud, long, stinky fart.

The boy happened to be nearby and smelled and heard the trump. He exclaimed, "By my Willie! What a fucking nasty stench!"

His father shouted out, "What did you just say, boy? Woe to you when I get out of here!"

"Sorry, Father!" Nasruddin replied. "I thought you were Mom!"

MORE DURABLE

Whenever young Nasruddin sat down in class, he used to pull down his pants and expose his buttocks before taking his seat.

When his teacher asked him the reason, he explained, "Because the skin of the buttocks is more durable than the fabric of my britches!"

OUT WITH A WHITE FACE

Young Nasruddin's mother wanted a large amount of yogurt, so she sent him to market to get some. He bought a full bag of curds in an unwieldy sack and hoisted it on his back. As he walked, the yogurt in the bag kept swaying from side to side, making it difficult for the teenager to carry.

"Stay calm, you crazy sack, be steady on my back," Nasruddin warned the yogurt. "You'd better stop shaking and making trouble for yourself — or you'll be sure to get my cock in you!"

Finally, the yogurt bag stayed put long enough for Nasruddin to walk home. When he got back, his mother told him to drain the yogurt by hanging it in the cloth sack. So the boy went out to the backyard and tied the bag on a low branch of a tree to strain out the moisture.

By now, Nasruddin was tired and decided to take a quick nap while the sack was draining, so he stretched out comfortably next to the tree. When not even a half-minute later, the yogurt started to drip down on him, he looked up and yelled at the bag.

"You rascal, I told you to behave!" yelled the boy at the bag. "If you don't settle down right away and stop interrupting my nap, you'll have the Devil to pay."

The yogurt did not answer but continued to drip on Nasruddin, swaying back and forth just ever so slightly in the breeze.

Furious, Nasruddin lowered the bag, tore a hole in the sack, and stuck his cock in the curds. Since the boy had no self-restraint and it felt good inside, he screwed the bag until he came.

When the overexcited young man withdrew his cock from the sack, he saw that it was thickly coated with yogurt. Then he exclaimed, "Truly, my friend, you have been in quite a few holes! But never before have I seen you come out from one with a white face!"

FELL OUT OF BED

One night, young Nasruddin's father, Yousef, was sleeping with a servant on a high bed. Hoping for a bit of a view of the two together in action, Nasruddin slipped up on to a corner of the bed just as the two were getting busy, but his father heard something, and called out, "Who's there?"

Nasruddin replied, "Just me!"

"And what are you doing here?"

"I was asleep and fell out of bed."

"You vile little liar," Yousef exclaimed, "when someone falls off the bed, then this is done from the top down, not from bottom up."

"Isn't it strange, Father," said the boy, "I was just wondering how that might have happened myself."

BIG FISH, LITTLE FISH

One day, young Nasruddin's mother, Leyla, was cooking and speaking to her husband, Yousef, as the child watched them unseen through a hidden crack in the door.

Leyla said, "Listen, my husband, I have prepared both a large and a small fish. We will hide the big fish under the wooden bench and serve the little one on the table to eat."

The father understood. "So, when the boy then has eaten and gone to bed, we will take out the big fish and eat it all ourselves."

A few minutes later, Yousef called Nasruddin in the other room, "Come on, boy, let's eat dinner."

He entered the room and sat down with his parents. When Leyla put the little fish on the table, Nasruddin grabbed it and held it to his ear.

Yousef shouted, "Hey, put that down, you little stinker! Why are you doing that?"

Nasruddin said, "I am sorry, Father, but I have to ask the little fish for some important information."

"And what is this critical matter about which you must ask the fish?"

"I want to ask him the name of the big fish that swallowed Jonah," answered the boy, innocently.

Since it was a biblical question, they indulged his silliness. Yousef said, "Ask your query quickly!"

Nasruddin whispered a short question to the little fish, then held it to his ear, listening intently. After a moment, the boy replaced the fish on the table platter and stared at it, arms crossed, with a dubious expression.

"Since you've already shared your question with us," Leyla said, "why don't you tell us the answer the little fish gave you?"

The boy said, "Well, the fish replied that he himself did not know. But under the wooden bench, he informed me, there is a fish that is bigger, older, and wiser than him, and he said that I should ask his friend that question!"

Two loaves of bread

Whenever Nasruddin's father wanted to fuck the boy's stepmother, Kerima, the boy's presence disturbed her. So, when he was old enough, she said, "You wretched child! All the children of the village have already made the *hajj*, the pilgrimage to Mecca, except for you."

He replied, "Wait — I'll go, but give me something so I can make the pilgrimage!"

She said, "By God, my son! I have nothing to offer you but these two small loaves of bread!"

Nasruddin took the bread and quietly walked out of the house as if he were leaving on hajj, but then he sneaked right back home. Undetected by his mother, he slipped into the house and hid under the bed. When Yousef returned home and asked where the boy was, Kerima said, "Praise Allah, he's left for the hajj!"

Yousef cried gleefully, "Now that the house is quiet, we can finally fuck each other in peace!"

While he busied himself between her legs, he asked, "Tell me, who do you think I am?"

Kerima said, "It is as if you were a judge of fifty years!"

Then he shouted, "Whoever needs a verdict, whoever has been a victim to injustice, must appear before the judge!"

Right then, Nasruddin crawled from under the bed and cried out, "I have been wronged, Your Honor! Please examine my case! Do you think it is fair that I should be forced to perform the pilgrimage to Mecca from here, with only two measly loaves of bread?"

CONTINUOUS FLOW

O nce young Nasruddin had to pee badly and went to the public toilet. Right next to the restroom was a fountain with loudly splashing water, so even after he finished pissing, he thought that it was not over yet. Finally, someone came up to the toilet and called out, "Hey, boy, why are you taking so long?"

Nasruddin replied, "I hear that my flow has not yet ceased, so I can not get up and go away until I finish peeing."

DON'T LET HIM DROWN

N asruddin's father, Yousef, took the boy to the Akşehir River to bathe. As Yousef waded out in the water and his penis was just about to be submerged, the boy cried out, "Father! Raise your pecker, so he does not drown in the water! Otherwise, you will have to give Mother the blood money for a reported murder."

FIGS AND RAISINS

N ight and day, young Nasruddin would make up fanciful stories, pose in silly faces, and tell asinine jokes, all of which drove his mother, Leyla, crazy. Although the boy was in truth quite clever, she was indeed much smarter.

One day Leyla called the boy and gave him a bolt of fabric, which she had spent more than a week to weave. "Bring this cloth to the dyer, and tell him he should color it a beautiful spring green."

Nasruddin took the roll of fabric and, not knowing the location of the dyer, carried it across the countryside. After an hour of walking, he became tired and sat down to rest in the shade of a cedar tree near a small pile of rocks.

While he was relaxing, a pretty lime-green lizard came and played among the stones. "Oh," said the child, "what a lovely green cloak you're wearing! Surely you must be the dyer. Listen, my mother told me to tell you that you should dye the fabric a beautiful light green, like your pants. In a few days, I'll be back to fetch it." Thus believing to have made himself clear to the amphibian, Nasruddin left the fabric on the stone pile and walked away.

When he got home, Leyla asked him, "What have you done with all the fabric I gave you to have dyed?"

"Mother, in the middle of the field stood a rock pile, where I met a man who wore a green coat so fine that I thought it must surely be the dyer, and so I gave him the cloth."

"No, you stupid child," cried Leyla "Who told you to leave it like that? Go down there right now again and do not come back home without that fabric."

Nasruddin ran back to the stone pile, but the cloth was nowhere to be found. "Hear me, little green dyer, give me my stuff back, or I will destroy your house," cried Nasruddin. The lizard, however, had long ago crawled away and did not reappear.

So, Nasruddin began to kick the stones, shouting, "You cursed overgrown bug! I have entrusted you with my valuables, and now you must return them to me, or you'll regret stealing. I'll destroy your house." Yelling in anger, he jumped on and kicked at the mound of rocks, finally dislodging some of them. As he caught his breath, he saw, hidden beneath the stones he had kicked away, a small pot of gold coins.

"Since you obviously have stolen and sold the fabric," he declared aloud to the hidden lizard, "I will just take the money that you owe me." So Nasruddin took a small handful of the gold coins from the pot and put them in his pouch. He carefully stuffed some nettles and thorns atop the coins, and covered the treasure pot with leaves and branches, and then headed home hugging the pouch to his chest.

As he walked back, a thief saw him and taunted him, "Boy, tell me: what is in your bag that you clutch it so desperately?"

"*Aman*, woe is me," said Nasruddin.

"Why do you say, 'Woe!'?" the man asked.

Nasruddin replied, "Just look for yourself."

When the thief reached into the pouch, he pricked himself with the thorns. The boy shouted, "You want to know what I have here? Nasruddin has brought his mother a beautiful gift! Don't you think she will be pleased with these lovely thorns and nettles?" So Nasruddin evaded the fellow and continued home.

When he arrived, he called to his mother and spoke very quietly to her, "Here, look what I have brought you, Mother," and pulled out the gold coins.

When he explained about the pot of money, Leyla told him, "You must go right now and bring me the rest of the coins in the pot." So the boy ran back and retrieved the pot of gold and lugged it home, where his mother quietly took the treasure and, singing his praises while making sure he watched her, hid it in the pantry.

Leyla realized that Nasruddin would never be able to restrain himself from blabbing to everyone in the village that he had brought her a fortune. So she hugged him and said, "You have done well, my son. You must be hungry and tired. Now eat your dinner and go to sleep, and maybe Jesus Christ will come to you in your dreams and reward you with dried figs and raisins."

When Nasruddin lay sound asleep on his bed, his mother took the pot and concealed it under a floorboard beneath the stairs. Then she filled her apron with figs and raisins, climbed quietly onto the roof, and threw the fruit through the window by the boy's bed so that they landed in his mouth. Nasruddin tasted the delicious fruits and ate everything he could chew while still dreaming.

The next morning he declared, "Imagine that, Mother! Last night, just like you predicted, I dreamt that Jesus Christ threw down figs and raisins from heaven. Do you think it might be a reward for having found the gold?"

Leyla just said, "A miracle! It must have been figs and raisins from Jesus!"

Nasruddin then went out and, precisely as his mother knew he'd do, he told everyone in the village, "I just brought my mother a big pot of money that I found underneath a pile of stones."

In less than a day, the people who had hidden the money heard that the boy was talking about their stash. Naturally, they wanted it back and so one posed as a constable to to call on Nasruddin and his mother.

The thief dressed as a cop said, "Your son has told everyone that you have a pot of gold that he found, concealed in your pantry. Do you not know that one must deliver found money to the court?"

"*Ai vai*," cried Nasruddin's mother. "What an idiot! You don't really believe all this crazy talk from my witless son? He is a moronic troublemaker. I know nothing about a pot of money."

"Are you sure?"

"Of course, I'm sure. But if you don't believe me, check the pantry for yourself."

Luqman inspected the pantry and found no pot of gold coins.

"But Mother," cried Nasruddin, "do you not remember the pot of gold that I brought to you — the same night that Jesus Christ showered down figs and raisins from heaven into my mouth as a reward?"

"You see? Clearly, the child is a numbskull without the least bit of common sense," the mother said. "I have learned long ago to simply ignore most of the things he says as pure jibberish."

Luqman chuckled and said to Leyla, "Kids these days. Forgive me. You must be right. Your boy certainly has no idea what he's talking about," and went away.

EYE ON THE DOOR

Leyla had to take the laundry to the well, so she admonished her son, "When I go out, keep your eye on the door!" So after she left, Nasruddin lifted the door off the hinges, strapped it to his back, and went to his mother to show her. When she saw him, she cried, "You've got the door, stupid child, put on your back! Now strangers can easily walk right in our home! Let us run back to the house!"

They did not go directly in, but waited outside and listened. Two hooligans who had already looted several homes were now in the house. She made the boy climb up a tree with the door, then followed him up to silently observe what was going on. They could hear the thieves laughing as they divided up their stealings.

A few minutes later, Nasruddin whispered, "Mother, I must go pee!"

"What? Are you kidding?"

"I *really* have to."

She said, "No, don't! Hold it in."

"I can no longer hold it!"

"Well, then, go ahead and let it out already!"

So Nasruddin peed down the tree right on top of the house, but the robbers thought it sounded like light rainfall.

Shortly, Nasruddin said, "Mother, I have to do something else."

"No, you can't! Just hold it in."

"I cannot hold it another minute."

"All right, go on and do it, then." And Nasruddin pooped from the tree.

When the bandits heard it falling on the roof, one said, "What in Allah's name is falling on the roof now — manna from heaven? Or birdshit, perhaps?"

After a few minutes, Nasruddin whispered, "Mother, I can scarcely hold the door any longer!"

"Hold it up," the mother pleaded with him, "just hold it up a little while more!"

"But it's so heavy, Mother. I can't hold it up one minute longer," said Nasruddin finally.

His mother said, "Well, then, go ahead and let it fall," and down crashed the door. The startled robbers thought they were being attacked, and fled like the wind, leaving behind all their contraband.

When Nasruddin and his mother climbed down from the tree, they found all the money and loot that the thieves had stolen, and kept it for themselves. Thus they once again had success, despite the boy's stupidity.

THE YOGURT TREE

Young Nasruddin was sitting under a large poplar tree when his friend Hussein commented on how nice it was in the shade. Nasruddin looked up and agreed, "What a beautiful tree this is!"

Just at that moment, a raven, sitting up in the tree, shat and it dropped onto his face. Nasruddin noticed that something white had fallen on him.

Hussein asked, "Do you happen to know what kind of a tree this is?"

Nasruddin replied, "Can't you tell? Obviously, this is a yogurt tree!"

GONE GRAY

Young Nasruddin often quarreled violently with his elderly mother, and she scolded him, "You ungrateful little bastard! My hair has turned gray — only due to your constant contradicting and quarreling with me!"

"It may be true," the boy replied, "that your dispute with me has made your hair turn gray. But tell me this: who made you pull out all your teeth?"

DID HE HAVE HORNS?

One night, as Nasruddin left the house, he stumbled in the front yard upon a dead body. Annoyed, he dragged the corpse to the well in the back of the house and threw it in.

However, his father witnessed this, took the body out of the well, and hid it. Then he slaughtered a ram and threw it into the well.

The next day, when the wife and relatives of the dead fellow roamed the streets and were calling for him, Nasruddin came to them and said, "The well in back indeed has a dead man — but come, look for yourself whether it is the one you seek."

They went to his house. Once there, they lowered Nasruddin down into the well. When he saw the sheep, he called up to the woman, "Did your husband, by any chance, have horns?"

Then they all laughed at Nasruddin and went their way.

THE LATE SHROUD

O nce when the family's servant girl died, her father sent young Nasruddin to the market to buy a shroud for her. He stayed away a long time so that finally, someone else took the matter into his own hands and bought a covering, in which the girl was carried to the grave.

By the time Nasruddin finally arrived, the girl had been buried already, and everyone had left. So he went alone to the graveyard. As he walked among the graves, he called out, "Has anyone seen the grave of the Ethiopian slave girl, whose shroud I have with me here?"

BLANKET WORTH

O nce when young Nasruddin slept with his mother in the same bed, she let out a loud, smelly fart. Wanting to know if the boy had noticed, she asked, "Tell me, son, how much did your father pay for this blanket?"

He replied, "He bought this blanket for fourteen dinars. But if your nasty fart will stick to it, I assure you that it is worth no more than four!"

POT AND MEAT

N asruddin went on a trip with an elderly teacher, but they forgot to take a cooking pot. So, they traveled for most of the day, and when it came time to make dinner, Nasruddin said to his patron, "I'm hungry and want to cook some food for us. Please ask the women by the river washing clothes there for a pot."

His teacher agreed and went to the group of women. One woman saw him coming and told the group, "Stay quiet. Let me handle this guy."

When the teacher reached the group, he said to the woman, "Excuse me, kind daughter. My pupil and I are on a pleasure trip, but unfortunately we have neglected to bring a cooking pot. Can you make a small pan available to us so we can cook our meal?"

"Pleasure trip? Here is a pot ready to be filled with juicy meat, or whatever you are hungry for," said the woman as she bared her vagina before the elderly man.

Then he cried, "Wait, wait, good woman! I have a young pupil. Let me get him, and then he can take it!"

"Fine," the woman said. "Just come back when you're ready."

The patron returned to the Mullah, told him what had happened, and said, "She is waiting for us to come back there!"

Nasruddin agreed, and so they came back to the river. When they arrived, the only woman remaining was the one who came forward before. The teacher said, "Well, good woman, here I am again with my student. Please, now, give us the pot!"

Again the woman bared her pussy, saying, "Ah young man, this is the only pan that is ready now for your use."

Immediately, Nasruddin stepped toward her, pulled out his cock, and exclaimed, "Yes, that's it! Come on, that is exactly how I like my meat cooked! And even better, my hands won't get blackened from carrying the cooking pot."

LITTLE LUCK

Once young Nasruddin went with his father to the hammam. When he returned, he told his mother, "Mother! I swear by Allah, in the whole bathhouse, I could not see a smaller cock than that of my father."

Then she wept and said to him, "My son! Why should your poor mother not even this once have gotten a little lucky?"

PEGGED

Young Nasruddin talked a lot at night, which got on his stepmother Sena's nerves. After she nagged his father, Yousef planed a large number of thick pegs, which he placed around the house in different conspicuous places. When the boy noticed, he asked his father, "What are you doing with all those pegs?"

Nasruddin's father replied, "If anyone talks at night, I insert a big thick peg in their butthole!" So Nasruddin went right away to bed and did not utter a peep until after sunrise. When he awoke, he found his father and mother screwing.

Later that morning, Nasruddin asked, "Father! Did she talk last night?"

"No, she didn't."

"So then why did you stick that plug in her hole?"

AFRAID TO MISS IT

When one of young Nasruddin's brothers died, his mother told him, "Go now: buy a shroud and some balm."

However, the boy refused, saying, "I won't go. Send someone else."

When she asked him why he would not go, he explained, "I'm afraid that once I've left you'll start without me, and I'll miss the funeral."

I AM MY FATHER

Once as young Nasruddin entered the house late at night, he found his father's servant sleeping naked.

He knelt behind her and parted her legs. As he was getting ready to enter her, she woke up and called out, "Who is that?"

He replied, "Be quiet, my dear. Don't worry. I am my father!"

PRAYERS TO SHEIKH JAFAR

As a teenager, Nasruddin always wanted to fuck his father's second wife, Sena. But she refused and rebuffed him.

One day, he entered his house and saw his stepmother talking with the trash collector. He cried out, "By God, I'll tell my father!" and then ran out of the house.

The young man went to tell Yousef, who was working in the fields. When he found his father fucking the donkey in the irrigation ditch, the boy shouted, "By God, I'll tell my stepmother!" and ran away.

At dinnertime, Nasruddin sat down at the table with his father seated to his right and his stepmother on his left. Imperiously he regarded his mother once, and his father once. Then he turned to his father and asked, "Shall I tell her?" Immediately the ashamed father embroiled Sena in a lengthy conversation.

Finally, the boy turned to his stepmother and asked, "Shall I tell him?" But before she could engage Yousef in conversation, he became suspicious and said to the boy, "As for me, you have seen me, fucking the donkey in the irrigation ditch. But what did you see her do?"

Nasruddin blurted out, "By Allah, Father: I watched as the garbage man kissed her right here in the house."

Yousef was furious, rushed at her, slapped her, and threatened her with divorce. Later, when they were alone, Sena cried, "It's untrue. The boy is jealous because I've refused his advances. First thing tomorrow, I will go to the tomb of Sheikh Jafar to pray to make the boy go blind."

Nasruddin was listening very carefully and heard everything.

The next morning Nasruddin left the house before his stepmother and ran to the mausoleum of the great Islamic leader, Sheikh Jafar. The boy was safely hidden behind the coffin when his stepmother arrived. She bowed reverently, knocked on the coffin, and called out, "Oh Sheikh Jafar, please bless me and grant my single prayer."

"Pray tell, my child," Nasruddin answered her in a ghostly voice from behind the tomb, "what is your prayer?"

"Oh great Sheikh, if it is in your power, then you must make my lascivious stepson go blind!"

"It is possible . . . but there is a sacrifice you must make."

"But what is required?" she implored. "I swear, I will do whatever is needed."

Sheikh Jafar answered, "You must give the boy to eat, every day for forty days, two dark chickens — then his eyes shall fail, and he shall go blind." Sena thanked the saint and took the dust of his tomb. She hurried to the market and then home to kill and cook two fat dark chickens. When Nasruddin came home, she immediately sat him down and served him the two roasted dark-meat fowls, and he devoured them.

So it continued, each day for forty days, Sena gave him two dark chickens to eat, until at last, Nasruddin complained that he could hardly see anything. Now he never left the house, peed and shat in bed, and his mother had to take him from bed to toilet and guide him around from one place to another. Finally, she complained to Yousef, admitting, "I'm to blame that the boy has gone blind because I asked at the tomb of Sheikh Jafar to make him so. But now, I regret it completely."

Nasruddin's father instructed her, "You should return to the gravesite of Sheikh Jafar in the morning and ask him to reverse the curse. Maybe he will restore Nasruddin's sight, and you can regain some peace."

Sena sighed with relief. "Yes, tomorrow first thing I will go there."

Nasruddin overheard the whole thing.

Early the next morning, the boy slipped away from the house and ran to the tomb. Shortly after he was situated, hidden in the back of the coffin, his stepmother entered. Hands clasped in obeisance, she piously approached the saint's crypt and cried out, "Oh Sheikh Jafar! I was wrong. I must repent my previous prayer, which blinded my young son. Now I want to pray that you can do something to make the boy open his eyes and see again like before."

Nasruddin answered her in a spectral voice from behind the coffin, "It is possible . . . if you can make up your mind . . . but it will require additional sacrifice."

"Fine, please just tell me what to do to make it right."

"Now you must give him to eat, every day for forty days, two light chickens — then he shall see once more," commanded Sheikh Jafar.

So she thanked the saint for hearing her prayers, went home, and for forty days, each day, fed him two roasted light-meat chickens until his sight was finally restored as before.

The next day, Sena ordered the boy out of the house on a ploy. "You stink, boy. Now that you can get around yourself, take your things, go to the hammam, and stay there for at least two hours until you are clean from head to toe." He understood that she wanted him out of the house so she and his father could fuck in privacy, so he took his clothes, went to the baths, washed and dressed quickly, and rushed home again. Finding no one in the house, he hid under the bed.

Soon his parents returned home and called for him. Sena said, "I told him to go to the hammam."

Yousef exclaimed, "Praise Allah! Now that the house is quiet, we can finally fuck in peace." He took his wife, laid her on the bed, and spread her legs. He was just about to mount her when she said, "Wait . . . I have an idea. Why don't we give my vagina a name, and you must give your pecker a name. That way, we can talk about fucking in front of the child without him knowing."

"That is a fine idea, my love," he said. After a moment, he suggested, "So then I'll name my penis 'The bloated corpse'."

She said, "Perfect. And so we can call my pussy 'The open grave'!"

He declared, "Excellent. Now it is time to bury the big bloated corpse in the open grave!"

Suddenly Nasruddin jumped up from beneath the bed and shouted, "There is no God but Allah, there is no God but Allah!"

Nasruddin's father yelled, "What are you doing, boy?"

Nasruddin just stood in front of him and replied, "Father! Surely you have not forgotten that a righteous Muslim does not bury the dead without calling out, 'There is no God but Allah!'?"

DON'T PULL HIS LEG

One day, Mullah Nasruddin went to the tailor to buy a pair of trousers. He found a pair that he liked so much that he decided to wear them home. Some of Nasruddin's friends noticed his new pants and schemed to play a trick on him. So they distributed themselves in his path along the way home, and the first person he met, said after they greeted each other, "What do you want with those pants, Mullah? You don't need them. Give them to me."

The Mullah said, "Go away, and leave me alone!" Five times the same scenario was repeated between him and one of his friends. Finally, when Mesut came forward, Nasruddin acted as if he had been convinced. He stretched out his leg and said to Mesut, "Come on, then — take it!"

The other man bent down to pull his trouser leg, but the Mullah gave him a kick in the rear, which sent the fellow face-down in the dirt. Nasruddin announced to all the men, "Now, I hope, you have learned who I am, and now you know that I am the one who pulls the pranks around here."

THE NEW ONE

When Nasruddin was a teenager living with his parents, and his mother had gotten older and started losing her figure, his father Yousef announced that he wanted to marry a second, younger wife. Yousef's friends and neighbors said to him, "Why must you do this? Nasruddin's mother is a good woman."

"I need a young bride," said Yousef, "to hold together my old bones!"

People admonished him, "May God grant you happiness, but please — change your mind!"

Nasruddin's father replied only, "I shall not be denied." So he chose and married a shapely young woman, Sena, and took her home where she lived together with Fatima and Nasruddin. Since she was the new wife, the old man was as pliable as a piece of dough in her hands. She drove Nasruddin and his mother almost crazy, so that soon they were, as they say, "seeing stars in the midday sky."

Finally, Nasruddin decided that enough was enough. "By my Willie," he told his friends one day, "I will teach that woman whose house this is!" So he came up with a plan.

The next day, when Yousef left his shoes outside the mosque to pray, Nasruddin stole and hid them. Naturally, a few days later his father bought a new pair of shoes that he brought home.

The following day, his father called the boy, saying, "Nasruddin, go fetch my new footwear, for I will go to the mosque!"

Nasruddin asked, "The old or the new?"

"The new, of course."

"Your old pair of shoes, you mean?"

"No, you meathead, the new one. Someone took my old pair of shoes. So, get me the new pair of shoes."

"So you mean the new pair, or the old pair?"

"The new one. The new!" yelled his father.

So Nasruddin ran to Sena and told her, "Father has told me to fuck you!"

She was astonished and replied, "What did you say, you little pervert? I can scarcely believe those words came out of your father's mouth, let alone yours."

But Nasruddin just stuck his head through the door and yelled, "Hey, Father, I forget. Did you tell me, the new or the old one?"

Yousef shouted back angrily, "You little fool. If I've told you once, I've told you a dozen times, the new one. The new!"

Then Sena had to comply with Nasruddin's father's wishes.

THE CORRECT CURSE

Young Nasruddin and his mother were arguing about the boy's house chores when he lost his temper and started screaming at her. Leyla went weeping to her husband and told him, "Your son has forsaken his poor mother and cursed me to the Devil."

But when Yousef went in his son's bedroom to confront him, he acted quite composed and unconcerned about anything. He pulled the boy's ear to get his attention, then scolded him. "You little scoundrel. Did not the Prophet command in the Quran to all true believers to respect their parents, saying, 'Then do not say "Ugh!" to them'?"

Nasruddin calmly replied, "Indeed, Father, it is true that the Prophet has spoken the truth. But honestly, I did not say, "Ugh!" to her, nor did I even say "Huh!" All that I said to her was this: "You skanky whore, you cunt, you scumbag, you bitch."

THE DARKENING PLACE

Once young Nasruddin was with his father in the bathhouse and observed that the beard of his father was gray. Then he looked at his father's cock and saw that it was very dark. So he asked, "Why is your cock so dark?"

His father replied, "Because he's been buried so often in your mother's vagina."

Nasruddin suggested, "Then why not stick your long gray beard into mother's vagina, and it will become darker too?"

ALWAYS BE PREPARED

One day Nasruddin was talking with his buddies about where they should take a walk. He suggested, "Let's go to the river and watch the women bathe." The others agreed and followed him.

As the young men approached the river, one of the women bathing on the other side noticed that she was being observed, and she continued to undress, facing the boys. When she revealed her vulva, Hussein teased him, "Nasruddin, will you not grab the opportunity with both hands?"

Without hesitating Nasruddin opened his robe, pulled out his prick, and called, "Look, my comrades! One should never take me for unprepared. Like a tree, I have to stand ever ready at service to my friends, always ready to provide a sturdy branch onto which anyone can climb."

DESTINED TO DIE

As young Nasruddin's father once was seriously ill, they sent him to fetch the doctor. But instead, he went to the undertaker, and told him, "My father is dead. Come with me to wash him."

The mortician went with the boy to the house. When he found Nasruddin's father weak but still quite alive, he said, "Nasruddin, your father's still living."

Nasruddin replied, "You're right. But I was certain that, by the time you finished washing the body, he was already destined to be dead."

So the undertaker laughed and went his way.

SEPARATE THE WHEAT FROM THE BARLEY

Nasruddin was quite young when a merchant traveling through Akşehir taunted him, "I bet you're too stupid to count on your fingers."

The boy said, "Well, try me."

The man said, "Okay then, first, take two sacks of wheat." The boy carefully closed both his pinky and ring fingers.

"And then take two sacks of barley." The boy bent his forefinger and thumb down, which of course left his middle finger, pointing out. The man acted offended and asked, "Why do you let the middle finger stick out like that?"

Nasruddin replied, "So that the wheat does not mix with the barley."

THE PILE IN THE VINEYARD

Young Nasruddin was passing a vineyard and was very thirsty, so he jumped the fence and began to pull down and gobble the delicious grapes. But Bekri, the owner, spotted him and yelled, "Boy, what in Allah's name are you doing?"

"I came here to empty my bowels," said Nasruddin innocently.

Bekri said, "And just where did you leave your little gift of manure?"

The boy looked all around but saw nothing with which he could justify himself. Finally, he spotted a mound of donkey manure and declared, "There it is."

"Do you take me for a fool? That's a pile of donkey dung," said Bekri.

Unruffled, Nasruddin replied, "If that heap is neither from you or from me, then I really have no idea from whom or what it might be."

THE USUAL TIME

After Nasruddin's father died, his mother cried a lot. One night, she was in her bed and weeping. Nasruddin asked, "Why are you crying, Mother?"

She replied, "I'm sad and lonely. When I thought of your dear departed father, I felt a sharp pain in my belly."

"Of course," said Nasruddin, "that explains it. Now is the usual time when he would have fucked you."

SHOE RETURN

Once as a young man, Nasruddin was performing his ablutions — his ritual prayers while bathing — on the shore of Akşehir River. As he was washing his left foot, he noticed his shoe floating away. He lunged forward to catch it, but it was too late. His pointy shoe was heading downstream in a hurry.

At first, Nasruddin did not know what to do, but then he became so enraged at the brook for stealing his shoe that he turned his back to it and loudly broke wind. Of course, in Islamic religious culture, passing wind while performing a sacred rite of prayer is a vile act that invalidates the ritual.

Nasruddin then stood upright, faced the stream, and shouted, "Oh river! I gave you back your ablution. Now — give me back my shoe!"

DAMNED IF YOU DON'T

One day as a young man, Nasruddin was arrested by the town watchman, Luqman, and brought before Bekri the judge. Luqman reported, "This pervert was publicly masturbating in an alley just off the town square." The judge threw Nasruddin in jail for a day.

The next morning, after his release from behind bars, Nasruddin went to the chai shop. As he took his seat, Abdul asked him how he was doing. Nasruddin replied, "My story is just too marvelous. On the one hand, they will not allow us to fuck each other. And on the other hand, when we fuck ourselves, they lock us up."

WHAT THE CROW TOLD

Young Nasruddin was passionately in love with his stepmother, Sena, who was, in fact, closer in age to him than to his father. Several times, he approached Sena, trying to seduce her into bed, but she steadfastly refused him, for she was a pious and devoted wife and expressed no desire to do anything forbidden. So he got nowhere with her.

In desperation, the boy forged a letter from Sena's father that he sent to his father by way of a farmer. The message began: "First, a warm greeting to Yousef."

Then it continued: "Effendi, this very hour, as soon as this letter arrives, send to me my daughter, Sena, because of some important issues about her mother's health that I must discuss with her."

When Yousef read Sena the message from her father, she stood up at once and said to him, "Take me to my father, or divorce me and set me free!"

He replied, "As for me, I cannot take you. And as for the boy, I fear for your virtue. If it were not for that, I would send you with him."

She said, "Not all males are created equal, Yousef. I swear, nothing at all will happen on the trip. I swear, I will not even talk to the boy along the way."

When the boy appeared before his father, he commanded him, "Boy! I wish that you would be kind enough to bring your stepmother to her father's house. But if anything untoward should happen, you'll have the Devil to pay!"

Nasruddin said, "Today we can't travel, Father. The donkey must be washed, fed, and rested before the trip. But tomorrow, I'll take her to her father's house."

The boy walked to the stable, but instead of grooming the donkey, he grabbed a large sack with several items that he had stashed there earlier, then slipped out of the stable unnoticed and ran down the road toward Sena's father's home.

About midway there, on an empty stretch of the road they would take the next day, Nasruddin stopped. From the sack, he produced a sweet juicy watermelon, two spoons, and a knife, and hid all of that beside a tree where a crow was sitting. Before he left there, he threw a couple of stones at the bird, which made it caw.

He turned toward home and walked a third of the distance back until he found a tree with a peaceful crow in it. He took sweets and dried dates from his sack and buried the food beside the tree. Then he threw rocks at the bird until it squawked.

Then he continued half of the rest of the way home, where he spied a large tree where a crow perched calmly. He took a fish, a frying pan, bread, radishes, and limes, and hid them carefully behind the tree. Then he threw a stone at the bird to make it caw.

At last, he ran back home and washed and fed the donkey before he ate a quick dinner and went to sleep.

Early the next morning, he put Sena on the donkey and walked behind her on the road in silence. Not long after, she complained to the boy about her hunger, admitting that she was unprepared without any provisions for the journey. So young Nasruddin told her, "Blessed is the virtue of patience! The journey should take only a short distance."

She said, "Don't try to trick me, boy. I know this road very well, and I am certain that we have gone only one-sixth of the way to my father's house."

"As you say, dear stepmother."

Suddenly a crow squawked in a tree nearby. Nasruddin threw a stone at the crow and shouted at it, "You lie, you dog!" He kept walking, ignoring the bird.

The dark bird croaked a second time, and the boy stopped and said, "What? Unbelievable! You can't possibly be telling the truth."

Sena asked, "Are you out of your gourd, boy? Why are you talking with that bird? How do you know its language? What does it say?"

Fuming, Nasruddin said, "Oh, it's just stupid bird babble. The crow told me an incredible bullshit story. He said, 'There are, child, under that tree, tasty radishes, limes, fish, bread, and a frying pan.'"

"Oh, stop your foolishness. That's absurd. How can you even understand it?"

Nasruddin folded his hands and said, "I once read in the Book of Solomon, son of David — may peace be attained by reading about him — and I have become fully conversant in the languages of birds and wild animals."

"Well, I don't know about that, but look around the tree, for my sake," she said. "Maybe, just maybe, it's true."

Reluctantly, Nasruddin went to the tree and looked around the back of the trunk, and from underneath an outgrown root, he brought out the fish, bread, radishes, and limes.

Thinking this was some fabulous miracle, Sena was astonished as much as she was famished. She slid off the donkey to kiss his hands, pleading that they stay there to eat. He took his hands back to cook the meal, and together they ate until they were well satisfied.

Then the boy lifted her back upon the donkey as he walked alongside, and they went a few miles further until there croaked a raven on a tree. Nasruddin threw a rock at the bird and shouted, "Scram, you miserable piece of crap! Stop telling me your ridiculous lies."

Sena said, "He's not lying. We have tested his sincerity. What does the blessed raven tell now?"

"Unbelievable. That stupid crow says that under this tree, there are sweets and dried dates." She asked him to go and look, so he went and dug a little, and shortly he produced another platter with many tasty treats. He lifted her off the donkey onto the ground, and they both ate the delicious sweets and fruits.

Nasruddin sat behind her on the donkey, and they rode together silently for some time until she became thirsty. She complained, "Nasruddin, my throat is parched now. Do you see our dearest friend, the crow, about? Perhaps he can tell us where we can find a drink of water. Can you find him?"

He quietly replied, "Be patient, my dear stepmother. We're almost there."

After a while, on an otherwise desolate area, they came to a single tree where there was a crow. When they stopped before the tree, the crow cawed sharply, whereupon he said, "You lie, you nasty dog!"

Sena argued, "By God, sir, I recognize our raven. The blessed bird speaks the truth. He has proven his trustworthiness a second time. So now, please, you must tell me what he says."

Nasruddin said, "I see no reason to believe that deceitful bird, but what he told me was: "Near that tree, you will discover a juicy watermelon, a knife, and two spoons.'"

"I beseech you, in Allàh's name," she said. "Go quickly and follow his instruction, for I am so incredibly thirsty."

So he went to the tree, dug around the roots, and brought out the melon, knife, and spoons. They sat down, he split the melon in half, and both quenched their thirst with the juicy fruit. Sena was now completely crazed with affection for Nasruddin and kissed his hands and feet repeatedly.

He sat her back up on the donkey again, and before he mounted behind her, he threw another stone at the raven. It cawed a long time again, and the boy, seemingly shocked, yelled up at the bird, "You lying, filthy, horrible creature, damn you!" And he threw yet another rock at the bird, provoking another feather-fluttering squawk.

"By Allah! Behave yourself, or you'll get a taste of my shoe!"

Sena objected, "Wait, Nasruddin, do not attack him. By God, this most fortunate and helpful of birds does not lie; he speaks the truth. We have witnessed it once, twice, and even a third time. In his honesty, what does the crow tell us now?"

Nasruddin shamefully replied, "Please, shut up! Don't even ask. What this foul-beaked bird tells me now are shocking and immoral words that I cannot even pronounce. And even if I could articulate his unthinkable suggestion, I would rather slit my throat than put it into practice. Do not ask me to speak another word about it."

He mounted the donkey and sat behind Sena. She was silent for a while, but then she could not bear to wait another moment to understand the raven's unique message. She begged her stepson with profound oaths of loyalty and obeisance until the boy finally relented and revealed, "That nasty bird told me this heinous message: 'You must lie down with your stepmother and take her fully — once, twice, and three times. And if you do not, then it is fated that your young step-brother will die a slow, torturous death and be sent to Hell.'"

Sena broke down in tears and wailed without restraint, "I pray to thee, by the mercy of Allah.! What a wretched predicament! Misery is to be my destiny. Your stepbrother is my only child — I have no one in this mortal life but him. So although the remedy is unspeakable, you must not be the cause of his death."

Nasruddin said with disdain, "I can't believe you would even consider such a proposition. You may not have any morals, but I find it disgusting and degrading — I'll never do that."

She implored him now with oaths and vows of love, and kissed his hands and face for several minutes, finally ending in a full-mouth kiss. He pulled her off the donkey and down to the ground, and there on the side of the road, three times he fucked his stepmother. Then he brought her to the residence of her father and left to ride his donkey contentedly home.

Later, after she returned from her father and family, she confessed to her husband the whole story from beginning to end.

Yousef understood everything and screamed at Sena, "You let him fuck you? Three times? Don't you understand? The boy tricked you, you whore, so that he could fuck you."

He abused her, then proceeded to divorce her, and swore never to marry again. He sent her back to her father with a letter that declared, "Now that whore is no longer my wife. So if anyone ever says to me, 'Nasruddin has fucked his mother,' it will not be valid anymore."

PART III

Extra-Marital Affairs

NEW WINE IN AN OLD WINESKIN

In his late teens, Nasruddin's nosy neighbors Hussein and Setare were visiting his parents for coffee one afternoon. They teased him for remaining a bachelor for so long. "You should get married already," admonished Hussein.

Nasruddin replied, "I swear, I will not marry until the river brings me a woman."

Setare asked, "How can the river bring you a woman?"

"I declare to you: this is how it will be!"

One week later, Nasruddin was bathing in the river when he saw a rather plain middle-aged woman approaching him. He covered himself in a towel and went up to the stranger and asked, "Who are you, and where are you from?"

She smiled sweetly and replied, "My name is Fatima, and I'm from Konya."

"Where are you going?"

"I've decided that I want to go to this town here."

"What will you do here if you like it?"

"If I like it and can find a husband, I will stay and live here."

"Do you have children?" Nasruddin asked.

"Nay, I have none now."

"Have you ever had one?"

The woman bowed her head and said quietly, "Yes, I had an infant son who died in his father's arms ten years ago, when our home caught on fire and burned down to the ground while I was away our from home, taking care of my sick mother."

"I cannot be your husband. You are sure to bring the child's misfortune to us."

"But Sir, I think I might like it here. How can one carry forward the illness of a child who died before his first birthday?"

Nasruddin had no immediate response to that, so after a long awkward pause, he asked, "Would you like me to marry you?"

"Yes, I would."

They joined hands and entered the town and went to the elders to get married right away. After the wedding celebration, they moved in together into an old cabin. The two were happy until the end of the rainy season when all the men went out to work in the fields.

Early springtime one day, Fatima kissed her young husband goodbye for the day as he was preparing to leave, and she took the laundry to the river. Nasruddin happened to thump the floor and heard a faint metal rattling underneath the floorboards. He pried open the squeaky board and found a small jug, which jiggled when he pulled it up. He upended the jug and out fell a handful of gold coins, a modest but much-appreciated treasure.

With three coins, Nasruddin bought dates, bread, and butter. The rest of the gold he carefully put in an old wineskin, which he then tossed up on the roof for safekeeping.

The next day, not wanting to appear as if anything extraordinary had happened, he left in the morning, as usual, to work in the fields.

That afternoon, a traveling mendicant knocked on Nasruddin's door while Fatima was chatting in her front yard with her neighbor, Setare. The poor man, hands clasped in supplication, implored, "I am preparing for a long pilgrimage across the desert. Please give me an old wineskin that I can fill with water."

She answered, "Certainly, I'd gladly oblige, but I have none."

Setare pointed out, "But Fatima, there is on old wineskin atop your roof."

Fatima climbed up, retrieved the wineskin, filled it with water, and gave it to the penniless pilgrim. He wept in gratitude, "Thank you! God bless your children."

"I have no children," she answered. "I had one, but he died young."

"May God have pity and bless him and you," the beggar said as he left, taking the old wineskin, with the gold coins submerged below the water.

When he returned, Nasruddin climbed to the roof and discovered that the old wineskin in which he had hidden the gold was gone. So he climbed down and demanded of Fatima, "Where in Allah's name is the wineskin that was up on the roof?"

"A poor man came and asked me for a wineskin, for water," she answered. "Setare noticed the wineskin. So I went up to the roof, took the wineskin, and gave it to the unfortunate fellow. Before he left, he prayed for my deceased son."

Nasruddin yelled, "He was unfortunate, you say? Did I not predict that your dead son would come back to cause us harm? Instead, you said, 'How could a dead person harm us?'" Fatima was speechless.

Nasruddin went directly to the market and bought a new, large, beautiful wineskin. Then he went to where the beggars hung out at the edge of town and called out, "Who will exchange an old wineskin for a new one?"

One of the older beggars spoke up. "Here, I will. Take this nasty used wine-skin. Some stupid lady with a dead son gave it to me. I want a nice new one."

The Mullah exchanged the new wineskin for the old one. He got it back without the poor mendicant ever learning of its contents. Satisfied, he went back and rebuked and repudiated his wife.

No rest for the married

For a while as a young man, Nasruddin was a real night owl. One evening after another, he went out with friends to tell jokes and dance and sing and laugh. Often, Nasruddin did not return home until just before dawn. His father, Yousef, was very unhappy with this behavior and admonished his son, "What you need is to get married to a nice girl."

He put off his father, saying, "I'm not mature enough to settle down now and take a wife. There is plenty of time."

They went back and forth about this for many years until at last his father said, "Nasruddin, you are wasting your money and ruining your health! Why don't you marry? What about Mary? She would certainly be a good wife."

"Leave me alone," Nasruddin told Yousef. "I'm quite contented being a bachelor and am not in the least bit anxious to start a family." After many long arguments, however,the young man relented and agreed to find a spouse.

So he looked around for a compatible bride and found a single young woman who also enjoyed the nightlife, and they wed.

After four months of married life, you could almost not recognize Nasruddin, as weak and thin as a young sapling. He was exhausted from repeated, long lovemaking sessions to his wife. They kept each other awake all night long, every night of the week.

One afternoon while he was sitting outside in the garden, Nasruddin became sleepy and wanted to nap. He was not as vigorous as he used to be, although he had gained more pleasure in his frolicking. But for just a little time now, he needed to relax his bones and take some rest, so he leaned his tired frame against a shady tree and fell asleep.

Just then a fly landed on his forehead and did a little dance, buzzing and flitting around his face, doing all the irritating things insects do. Though Nasruddin swatted the bug away repeatedly, it kept returning to the top of his bald head. Naturally, he became annoyed and could not find the least bit of repose.

Finally, he screamed at the fly, "Shame on you! Get out of here and leave me alone, you awful bug! If not, then I'll have my father trick you into taking a wife and getting married. Then I'll bother you, and *you'll* know how it feels to be exhausted and have others forbid you even a moment of rest."

Don't show it to me

Fatima, Nasruddin's first wife, was wed to Nasruddin from a nearby village by arrangement at a tender age. As was the custom those days in her tribe, she did not reveal herself to her husband before the wedding.

On their wedding night after the ceremony, Fatima sat before her new husband, parted the veil for the first time, and showed him her face. Unfortunately, she was quite a homely girl (although it should be said that she became less ugly as a young woman and that Nasruddin himself was no prize). Nasruddin cringed.

The next day as they were walking, she asked, "Tell me, husband, in front of which of your male relatives may I take off my veil and reveal my face?"

"You may lower your veil and show your face to anyone you like," he groaned, "so long as you never show it to me."

Exactly what I would do

When Nasruddin was a newlywed, just on the third night, Nasruddin was dreaming he was swimming deep in a vast ocean. It was a happy dream until he woke up to realize that he'd accidentally wet the bed.

Of course, when he felt the dampness, he was embarrassed but unsure how to tell his wife, Fatima, snoring fast asleep next to him. So Nasruddin arranged his blanket partly over the damp spot and then lay back down, pretending to be asleep.

A minute later, he bolted upright with a loud gasp, "Arghhh! Dear Allah, save me, save me!"

Fatima awoke and turned to look at her husband. "What's the matter?"

The trembling and visibly shaken Mullah replied, "Fatima! Oh, my sweet wife, you have no idea what sort of horrifying nightmare I've just had!"

She asked, "What did you dream?"

"In my dream, I saw three tall minarets, one set right above the next, and atop the third minaret was an egg, and on that egg was a needle, and on that needle balanced a covered table, and at that table, I had to eat my dinner."

Fatima gasped, "How terrifying! What a predicament! My poor husband!"

Nasruddin replied calmly, "You won't believe how shocked I was."

Fatima sympathized, "My dear husband, I can only imagine. You must have been frightened out of your mind. Out of sheer panic or dread, I would have soiled the bed, or worse."

"Indeed," Nasruddin agreed, "that is exactly what I would have done myself."

OPEN-AND-SHUT CASE

One day Nasruddin went with his wife to the river to wash clothes. When she put her foot into the water, a scorpion grabbed one of her toes, and she screamed, "Help, Mullah, help!"

"Sit down," said the Mullah, "so I can see what kind of hellish creature it is." He bent down and looked to view what had grabbed her. But as he leaned forward to better see the animal, the scorpion grabbed his nose with its other pincer, so that now the scorpion had a grip on them both. Out of sheer terror, Fatima cut loose a loud fart. Then the Mullah declared, "It's not you who needs to open up — but the claws of this crab!"

NO TIME TO REST

When Fatima was pregnant, Mullah devotedly cared for her. But after nursing his wife for months, he told her: "My poor sick love! Please — let me go out and get some medicine and some fresh water for you."

She wept until the Mullah departed. Then she rose, hastily made the beds, swept the house, and cooked some food. Finally, after having put together the whole house, Fatima collapsed back into her bed and fell fast asleep.

When Mullah returned home and saw her passed out in the same position, he thought she had died. He gasped and clasped his trembling hands and ran to his wife's side. Laying his head upon her abdomen, he cried, "*Ai vai!* And now she's dead! My dear little boy, my dear little girl! Now you can no longer be born!"

FRIDAY MUST WAIT

One day, Mullah Nasruddin asked his wife, "Tell me, Fatima — what did the imam say today in his sermon?"

She answered, "He preached that a husband should fulfill his conjugal duties every Friday night as a religiously good deed."

The Mullah couldn't argue with that, so he agreed.

Fatima was very pleased with this arrangement, but the Mullah asked her, "I have so many business dealings during the week. How should I remember which night it is?"

Fatima countered, "Every Friday night, I'll always lay your turban on the dresser. That way, you will know what the right day it is for us to make love." Mullah agreed.

One Sunday night, Fatima wanted Nasruddin in bed again, and so she placed his turban on the dresser. The Mullah paused, but he felt obliged to take Fatima back to bed.

Two nights later, when Mullah came to bed, he saw the turban on the dresser and exclaimed, "Bitch! It is not Friday night!"

Fatima replied, "Silly man, today most certainly is Friday night."

The Mullah said, "We cannot continue like this for very long — either I must learn to wait for Friday — or Friday will have to wait for me! At this pace, I'll be a goner in no time."

AGE OR LOOKS?

In the chai shop one day, Abdul rushed in and cried, "Mullah, we need you now! Please, come quickly to our house. My wife and my sister are fighting each other — it has almost come to blows!"

"Relax, my friend. The matter cannot possibly be urgent. Sit down and tell me, what are the women fighting about?" asked the Mullah, unconcerned. "It can be only one of two things: their age, or their looks. Which is it?"

"Neither, really," replied Abdul, "not more than anything else."

"Then, my friend, go home and do not worry yourself," replied the Mullah confidently. "If it isn't about either of those two things, I am sure that their dispute will be over soon."

Ruin the Measurement

Fatima once asked Nasruddin, "Please go to the market to buy a yard of fabric." Nasruddin asked, "How long is a yard? This long?" He demonstrated the length by holding out his hands about even with his shoulders.

"No, it's this long," said Fatima as she adjusted his arms accordingly to correct the measurement. She went on to do other tasks, and the Mullah proceeded to leave. Getting outside proved a bit tricky until he realized that to get through the door holding his arms in their extended position, he had to turn sideways.

He continued comfortably like that for a minute, his hands stretched a yard apart, until he tried to pass someone in a narrow alleyway. As the fellow neared, Nasruddin yelled, "Get out of my way, you fool, or you'll ruin my measurement!"

Ride the Critter

One day Mullah Nasruddin was returning from the bazaar and decided to rest awhile on a slope next to the road. He took a melon from his saddlebag and sat on the stump of a tree to enjoy his food. As he was clumsily sitting down, however, the melon slipped from his hands and rolled down the hill.

Mullah watched as the melon rolled midway down the hill and smashed against the base of a bush under which a rabbit happened to be napping. The animal was startled by the noise and immediately took off the other way.

Nasruddin saw the hare bolt from the bush and pursued it downhill. He could not catch up, though, and eventually lost sight of the long-eared critter. Thirsty and angry, he headed back.

When the Mullah got home, he sat down and said, "Fatima, our melon must have been pregnant with a baby donkey. I dropped the thing, and it rolled and cracked open. Then I saw a tiny donkey — slightly larger than a cat with long floppy ears — run away. I gave it a good chase, but could not catch the thing. It ran as fast as an arrow shot from a bow."

"Pity!" replied Fatima. "Why did you let it escape, you lazy man? If only you could have caught the creature, I would love to have ridden it!"

The Mullah jumped up, grabbed a wooden spoon, and attacked his wife, shouting, "You whore! You godless woman! So, you want to mount a miniature donkey? You'd break its back!"

THE SLAVE BOY

Fatima had a handsome lover in the village named Ali. One day, he sent his well-built teenage son, Sedat, to take a message to Fatima that she should make herself up and get ready for him. She liked Sedat so much that she enticed him to stay and have some fun with her.

Moments after they finished, Ali knocked at the door, and Fatima hid her lover's son in the pantry. Then she took Ali to bed and fucked. Right after Ali and Fatima were done, they heard Nasruddin in the courtyard returning home.

One step ahead of the game, Fatima handed her older lover a large butcher knife and whispered, "Dress quickly! When the Mullah comes in, pretend to be rough with me and demand that I hand over your slave boy."

As Nasruddin entered the house, he saw Mehmet threatening Fatima, shouting, "Give me back my slave, you wretched cunt, before I cut you!"

Nasruddin immediately moved to protect her and yelled, "How dare you speak that way to my wife? You fiend, explain yourself before I throw you out of my house!"

Mehmet told him, "My slave boy has escaped, and I have reason to believe that your wife is hiding him in your house. You must release him to me now, so I can take him back and sodomize him."

Fatima confessed tearfully, "Yes, I admit it, his slave came here and asked me to shelter from the abuse of his master. I felt compassion for the boy, so I hid him in the pantry."

When Nasruddin opened the door to the pantry, they saw the young man crouching there. As Nasruddin profusely apologized for his wife's indefensible actions and pleaded for Mehmet's forgiveness, the man pulled the terrified boy by his cock and led him out the door.

THE THREE TALAKS

One day, sitting at the hearth, Nasruddin saw his wife's pussy and asked, "Fatima, tell me: what do they call that?"

Using a suggestive word for "inner flower," she replied, "*Talak*."

Now, *talak* is also a word that, if repeated thrice, is considered a solemn vow to end the marriage immediately.

"I divorce you," Nasruddin said, and pronounced the *talak* three times in a row, effecting their divorce.

"You stupid piece of crap," yelled Fatima, "what in Allah's name have you done? *Talak* is a flower!"

"You fucking cunt," shouted Nasruddin. "Do you think I should forfeit my right to superiority for your sake? I certainly wasn't about to give you the upper hand before I had the chance to divorce you."

ONE HOUSE IS PLENTY

One day, Fatima went to listen to the sermon at the mosque. When she returned home, Mullah inquired, "Tell me: what did the imam say today?"

She replied, "He declared that 'Whoever shall perform his marital duty to his wife, he manifests God, the Almighty, in His grace, and makes his home a Paradise on Earth."

That night before they went to bed, the Mullah declared, "Come, woman: let us build ourselves a house filled with God's grace," and they fucked.

A few short minutes later, Nasruddin rolled off his wife. She implored him to continue, "Mullah, you've just built a house for you. Hurry up, build me one, too."

Nasruddin kept his eyes closed, breathing heavy. He replied, "My love, it is easy enough to build you a lovely new house. But I fear that you will then eventually invite your father and your mother to live with us in, and then finally, you'll let all of your relatives into your fine new house, which will make the architect indignant. Please, do not grieve. One house between the two of us is plenty."

DARE TO STEP ON THAT

One day, Fatima noticed that Nasruddin was cutting his toenails and said to him, "Mullah, please bury your toenail clippings in a place where no one will step on them."

So he collected all his nail cuttings in the middle of the room, then dropped trou and took a crap on top of the pile. Fatima yelled at him, "You moron, Mullah! Why in the world did you do that?"

"Oh, come on," said the Mullah. "Just go ahead and tread on that if you dare."

GOSSIPMONGER

Abdul, whose chai shop Nasruddin and his friends favored, said, "I must tell you, Mullah, about your wife, Fatima. She is such a loudmouthed gossipmonger. All day long, while you are away, working hard, she visits our wives and distracts them from their housework with endless chitchat and mindless prattle. And her voice is so whiny that we must cover our ears even if in another room —"

Nasruddin interrupted, "Oh really, is that so?"

"Indeed," said Abdul. "She's constantly sticking her nose into other people's business, and always going around from house to house in the neighborhood, spouting her unwanted, cockamamie opinions."

Nasruddin retorted, "Lies and slander! If that were true, at one point she surely would have dropped in at home to gossip with me at our house — and I can tell you, most assuredly, she has never done that."

Abdul continued, "Not only that, your wife wears the most garish make-up."

Nasruddin replied, "And why shouldn't she? It looks good on the whore."

"Still, you really should speak to your wife about being quiet and staying home more. It isn't proper."

"All right, that's enough," said Nasruddin as he finished his chai and stood up to leave. "I'll be sure to mention it to Fatima — the next time I run into her."

PRICED BY EXTENSION

One day as Mullah Nasruddin was walking through the bazaar, he saw a sword with a very high price tag.

He said to the merchant, "Effendi, tell me why this item is so costly."

"You have heard the legend of Zulfigar, the sword of the fourth Caliph Ali, have you not? If you wave this sword at your enemy, it will extend two meters, just like Zulfigar."

Nasruddin went home and grabbed the fireplace tongs, then returned to the bazaar. He placed the tongs on sale, asking an exorbitant price. When the merchant saw that Nasruddin had his item marked up three times the cost of the sword, he asked, "Mullah, why are these old dirty tongs so expensive?"

The Mullah said, "When my wife throws these tongs at me, they extend at least ten meters more than your sword."

COME TO LIFE AGAIN

Once Nasruddin asked his wife, "How does one truly know if a person is dead?" Fatima answered, "Foolish man, everyone knows that you are dead if your ears and nose are numb and as cold as a tombstone."

A few days later, Nasruddin went up into the mountain forest to chop wood, and after some hours he felt his ears and nose were very cold and numb.

He cried out, "Why, I must be dead," and fell to the ground.

Shortly some of Nasruddin's friends came by and noticed the Mullah lying on the ground. Faik asked, "Mullah, what are you doing down there?"

"I'm dead," he said.

"But Mullah — how can a corpse speak?" asked Hussein.

"I must be dead, I tell you," insisted Nasruddin. "Now kindly, if you will, go fetch the imam and muezzin, and remove my body from this foreign land."

So they brought the imam and the muezzin, and the group lifted their dear departed Mullah's lifeless body on the bier, and they carried Nasruddin to his burial.

Now it seems that in that town back in those days, the custom was for folks to go up on the roof to watch the procession when a dead person was carried through the street.

So, while traveling in his casket, Nasruddin lifted his head to look around. A beautiful woman was standing on the roof of a house, and when he saw her face, he got hard.

The woman saw his prominent erection and called out, "This dead man has come to life!"

Nasruddin grabbed his hard-on, threatening, "Anyone who doubts that I'm dead, or who tells a lie about me when I am in my grave, gets this in them!"

MEAT SHOPPING

Once, Mullah Nasruddin had to officiate a service in the next village. Before he left, he gave Fatima some money with instructions to buy a particular cut of meat to make köfte, a special dish, for their dinner that night. En route, she ran into her lover Ali and, thinking that they would not be interrupted by the Mullah, they returned to her house for some fun.

No sooner had Fatima and Ali gotten into bed and started getting busy than Ali's wife burst into the bedroom with town constable Luqman, and took them both adulterers to court. Judge Bekri heard the case and ruled that both Ali and Fatima should each be tied upside-down naked on the back of a donkey and paraded through town in disgrace.

Meanwhile, Nasruddin returned home and, not finding his wife there, went looking around town for her. As he was standing in the town square, Fatima came by, still riding upside-down on the donkey.

Nasruddin stopped donkey and rider and said, "At last, I found you. Where have you been? What happened to you?"

Fatima replied, "Don't get in my way. I've already been to two butcher shops looking for your ridiculous special cut of meat and haven't found it. I've only got two more butchers to try, and then I'll come home."

DON'T MIX WITH THE EGGPLANTS

One morning, Fatima was snuggling with her new lover when Nasruddin came home unexpectedly, toting thirty eggplants he bought on sale at the market. She managed to stow her lover in the pantry and dress in time to greet her husband.

Nasruddin handed Fatima the sack of eggplants, and she stored all but one of them in the pantry atop her nude lover. The last eggplant she carefully hid. Then she ran back to Nasruddin, crying, "Allah help me! One of the eggplants has become a man! Ali, the greengrocer, must be a magician."

The Mullah went to the pantry and saw the eggplants piled atop the stranger. Suspicious, Nasruddin counted the eggplants — only to find twenty-nine.

Conned by Fatima's cunning ploy, he grabbed the naked man by his cock and dragged him back to the market. He pushed the man before Ali, saying, "I demand to know why you tried to slip in a man instead of one of the thirty eggplants I purchased."

Ali, a quick-witted occasional lover of Fatima's, realized what had happened. He pulled the man aside by his cock and spanked him several times, saying, "You little shithead, it's about time you got back here. I've told you at least a hundred times that you belong with the turnips. Now, don't mix with the eggplants again."

Ali apologized to Nasruddin for his trouble, handed him another eggplant, and sent him on his way home, another satisfied customer.

WITH BOTH OF YOU

One morning, Nasruddin's second wife, Kerima, was scrubbing the floor of their house. As she bent over on her hands and knees, her husband looked at her and noticed her two holes. He exclaimed, "Woman! I see two sweet holes! How wonderful! I was not even aware that you have two of them. Tonight I will take you by both! And so to tease you, all day long, every time I speak, I am going to add the sentence, 'Tonight I will pleasure myself fully with both your holes'." Kerima smiled and continued cleaning.

Later that afternoon, there was a knock at the door. The Mullah opened it and found two handsome young men with their palms folded. One of them spoke, "Mullah, we are students on pilgrimage, Ayman and Ozgur. Will you kindly offer us your hospitality tonight?"

"Fine, I grant it to you," replied the Mullah as he led them in. "You are welcome to stay here overnight in the pantry, but do not come out until I open this door again." He shut the door on them, but they could still hear everything through the open windows. Then he spoke lasciviously to Kerima, "Yes, tonight I will pleasure myself fully with both of your sweet young holes!"

Not realizing that the Mullah's wife was there, the students thought he meant that he intended to fuck both of them. "Allah save us!" whispered Ayman to Ozgur. "The Mullah must be joking!"

Nasruddin had brought a plump goose home from the market, so he said softly, "My dear, come now, and prepare the meal. It is time to stick this long-necked goose on the spit!" Again he added loudly, "Tonight I will fill both of your sweet holes."

Ozgur whispered, "Indeed, you must be right! The Mullah is not joking! By all appearances, he will deal with both of us as he has suggested since we got here."

Ayman whispered, "What else could it mean? He keeps repeating that he will sodomize us both. We must take turns staying awake so that one of us can defend us from anything that could happen." So Ayman took his shift keeping vigil while Ozgur slept.

After dinner, the Mullah whispered, "Kerima, it is time to prepare yourself for bed." Again he added, "At last! Now I will pleasure myself fully with both of your sweet young holes!" Then he lay down in bed with his wife, spread her legs wide, and crouched over her.

He crooned to his wife, "Indeed! First, I will delight myself with this hole, and then satisfy myself with the other one, and then begin anew!"

Ayman, who was awake, was frightened and thought to himself, *I have no idea which one of us the Mullah wants first, but if he comes in here and sees me awake, no doubt he'll fuck me.*

Panicked, he quietly woke up his comrade and said, "Hurry, Ozgur! We must leave here immediately — before he can fuck either one of us!"

So the two boys laced up their bundles, crept out silently from the room, took the leftover goose off its hook, and fled the Mullah's house into the night.

A MIND OF ITS OWN

During one of Tamerlane's senseless tantrums, the tyrant commanded the executioner to hang Mullah Nasruddin. His wife, Fatima, came to the gallows along with the rest of the town to attend the hanging, Nasruddin noticed his beloved wife at the front of the crowd and became aroused.

Tamerlane noticed the unexpected tenting in Nasruddin's baggy trousers and remarked, "How amazing, Mullah, that you can react like that. At your age. At a time and place like this. In front of me."

"Your Majesty," Nasruddin replied, "the only reasonable explanation is that your mind, my wife's mind, and the mind of that thing down there, are one of a kind."

LIFE OF THE PARTY

There was a private party in the village to which everyone was supposed to bring their secret lover. Fatima was invited to the party by her lover, Ali. It so happened that Nasruddin also was also invited to attend by his lover, but she had to cancel at the last minute.

Immediately when Nasruddin entered the room by himself, Fatima walked up behind him and launched into a tirade against him, crying, "You scoundrel! You wretched husband! You leave me hungry with no support our children at home — only to attend lavish parties like this."

She dispatched Ali to find a judge so that she could divorce him on the spot. While they awaited the judge, several of their friends came around and tried to reconcile the two. Eventually, they got Nasruddin to vow never to go again to parties like that one, and Fatima agreed to forget the whole matter.

The two left the party and headed back home. Midway, Fatima stopped short and declared, "Nasruddin, since you have misbehaved badly today and shamed me, you have ruined my evening so far. I have decided I want to stay out tonight. I might return home. Or maybe not."

Feeling that he had already caused enough trouble, Nasruddin went home alone, and Fatima returned to the soirée to have herself a delightful time.

PARTY FAVORS

One day, Mullah Nasruddin decided to celebrate his wedding anniversary with Fatima at their house and invited some friends and neighbors to join them. But when it was time for the party to begin, Nasruddin was busy out back in the garden, and he lost track of time.

When the guests arrived, Fatima greeted them all, with great love and respect, but without her husband. Several times she wondered why the Mullah was absent but was too busy feeding everyone and catching up on all the latest gossip.

Meanwhile, many guests came into the house and ate all the delicious food. When Nasruddin finally showed up, they realized that they forgot to call him to dinner, but all the delicacies he had paid for were already devoured. So the Mullah stormed out of the house to sit in the backyard to sulk.

Sometime later, Fatima wondered about Nasruddin's absence. When she at last found him in the backyard, she brought him back inside. Hussein asked, "So, Mullah, to where did you wander off? Why did you leave your anniversary party?"

The Mullah retorted, "I had my reasons, but I'll say this much about the matter: whomever has eaten the anniversary feast today should also go to bed with the bride and taste that delicacy!"

FAST AND SLOW

Faik asked Nasruddin, "Tell us, Mullah: while observing a religious holiday, does kissing your wife break the fast for true believers?"

Nasruddin answered, "Strictly speaking, kissing one's spouse when newly wed definitely breaks the fast. The second year of the marriage, it's a toss-up. But most certainly, you do not break the fast after the third anniversary."

RELAY THE MESSAGE

One day Fatima went with Setare and a few of the neighbor women to the lakeshore to wash clothes. At the same time, the regional Governor happened to walk by there. When he saw the women bent over their washing, the tall man was seized by erotic desire and stared lasciviously at them, obviously aroused.

After a while, one of the women noticed the strange man leering at them and alerted the other women they were being watched. Fatima stood up and called to him, "Why do you look at us like that, you fucking pervert, with your burning eyes and bulging trousers?" and hurled insults at him until he left.

The Governor inquired about this woman and learned that she was the wife of Mullah Nasruddin. He called for the Mullah to come to his office and asked, "Is that woman your wife?"

The Mullah said, "I may not remember her name all the time, but I can assure you that she's my wife."

The Governor leaned forward. "Go and bring her to me."

"Sir if you don't mind me asking: exactly what do you want with her?"

"I just want to ask her something."

Nasruddin said, "Just ask me! I'll be glad to relay your question to her properly."

The Governor hesitated, then admitted, "I want to take a crap on her pussy."

Nasruddin dropped his baggy pants and pointed his thickening cock toward the Governor. "Why don't you just sit on this right now, and then I'll place it in her pussy later on your behalf?"

ADVICE AND CONSENT

One afternoon in the chai shop, Hussein asked Nasruddin, "In your learned opinion, Mullah, what kind of people do you think are more despicable: those who married before you did, or those who married after you?"

The Mullah said, "Both are despicable!"

Hussein asked, "What makes you say that?"

The Mullah replied, "I despise the people who got married before me because they poorly advised me to get married. And I am just as angry, justifiably, at those who have married after me, because they have not followed my advice! May the Devil take them all!"

THE EXILE

Once Mullah Nasruddin had a horrendous quarrel with Fatima. He cursed her and said she was "long in hair but short in brains," at which point she started throwing things at him.

Nasruddin escaped and fled to the cellar, shut the door behind him, and collapsed in a dark corner, brooding and depressed. He just sat there, and the minutes turned into hours, and the hours into days.

Finally, after several days, his servant went to the cellar to get some supplies and was shocked to find the Mullah hidden there. She cried, "Praise God, sir, we have found you. What are you doing here?"

Nasruddin replied, "After the last dreadful argument with my wife, I went into exile by myself, determined not to be tortured and never to return to my homeland."

The servant pleaded with the Mullah. "We all just absolutely died searching everywhere around the house for you."

Nasruddin replied, "If that's true, then the dead should just leave poor me alone to perish alone in this foreign land."

OLD FRIENDS

Late one night, Luqman, the town constable, came across Fatima as she was heading to her lover Ali's house. He asked her, "Aren't you afraid to be out alone at this time of night? Either a strange man or the Devil may try to take you."

Fatima breezily answered, "Most certainly, I am not afraid. If a man gets a hold of me, well — that's exactly why I left home tonight in the first place. And if Satan comes my way, well — we are already old friends."

CARRY THE LOAD

One day in the chai shop, Hamid said to Nasruddin, "Tell us your honest opinion: is it true that men with big cocks derive more pleasure from lovemaking?"

The Mullah answered, "Indeed, I know that such men carry the load while others obtain the pleasure."

TRUNCATED LOVE AFFAIR

Nasruddin returned home from a trip to Konya unexpectedly early to find his wife in bed with their neighbor, Ali. Mullah grabbed him, tied him up, and threw him in a trunk. Then he left to get his wife's father and family to come and shame her publicly.

Meanwhile, Fatima managed to unlock the trunk and release Ali. Then she got him to help her push a baby donkey into the box and close the lid.

Not even a minute later, Nasruddin returned home with his in-laws and brought them to the trunk. He threw open the lid, and the little donkey jumped up and ran away. The Mullah, astounded at his wife's magical, if not miraculous powers, was speechless.

Enraged at his accusations of infidelity, Fatima's family proceeded to thrash the Mullah and denounce him as a faithless husband, then left him bruised and battered to consider the matter by himself.

MALADY AND REMEDY

When Fatima was standing at the window one afternoon, she happened to see a well-built stranger pissing across the road. Noticing his endowment, she was seized with such erotic desire that her legs began to quake. She swooned, crying loudly, "Oh! Allah save me!"

Nasruddin rushed to Fatima's side and, seeing her pale and faint, he helped her to bed and said, "My love, what ails you? Why do you cry out as if a camel were stepping on your toes?"

She answered, trembling, "Some unimaginable malady has come over me. I feel this feverish burning deep in my belly!"

The Mullah said, "That sounds serious. My dear, tell me what I can do."

"Where is the big fellow that I have seen across the road? Maybe he knows a cure for my disease!"

So the Mullah went looking for the man and brought him to Fatima's bedside, where the visitor observed, "I am not a doctor but I can tell you this much: your wife is very ill!"

"I already know that she's quite sick," said the Mullah. "But what can you do to help her?"

The big man looked into Fatima's eyes and diagnosed her illness immediately. He turned to the Mullah and requested, "Please bring me a few cloves of garlic." Fortunately, they had some at home, so he gave the garlic to the fellow.

Presenting the appendage that had attracted Fatima's attention, the man rubbed the garlic along its length. He then inserted it into the place that was receptive to this remedy, and slowly retracted it. Again and again, in and out, he applied the salve to the wound.

While the healing process was thus underway, Nasruddin tapped on the man's shoulder and said, "Sorry to interrupt, but . . . if you had told me what to do, I could have managed to take care of her all by myself. This procedure is a healing approach which is not entirely unknown to me — except that I would administer it to the patient at a lower dosage."

ALMOST HALFWAY

Nasruddin and Fatima started on foot for a trip that would take four days. After they walked about three hours, he asked, "How much farther is it?"

Fatima said, "If we walk all day, the rest of today and tomorrow, that will be half the distance."

The Mullah smiled and asked, "Why didn't you just say that we are almost halfway there?"

JESTATION

Arriving home breathless and clutching his backside with both hands, Nasruddin called to his wife, "Fatima! Quick, woman, come help me!"

Fatima ran to him and said, "What's the matter, Mullah?" She helped him to lay down on the bed.

"You must go and find me a midwife right away!"

"Fine, I'll go get Setare, she's just a few doors down. But why in Allah's name do you need a midwife?"

"I have just been fucked by Bekri, the judge. The way my ass feels, no doubt he has gotten me pregnant, and I am about to give birth. So hurry and get the midwife now — before it is too late."

WHO AM I TO JUDGE?

One day in the chai shop, Mesut told Nasruddin, "You know, Mullah, that your wife has sex."

Mullah responded, "Well, isn't that obvious? I fuck her. What would I do with a wife, who couldn't be fucked?"

Hussein piped in, saying, "Oh Mullah! You just don't get it. We're telling you: strangers fuck your wife. She sleeps around. A lot."

Mullah replied, "Well, who am I to judge Fatima? I am neither her brother nor her father."

ONLY THING LEFT

One cold, rainy day, Fatima told her husband, "You stink, Nasruddin. Go to the hammam and wash your body properly."

Mullah went to the hammam, where he steamed, scrubbed, and bathed for hours. But on his way home, he was caught in a torrential downpour of hail. By the time the Mullah made it to the chai shop, he was soaked and pelted. The chai shop owner, Ali, asked why he was so disheveled.

"If you listen to your wife's dictates," Nasruddin answered, "first you must singe your skin in an overheated hammam. Then you must be soaked by the coldest rain and pelted by hail. The only thing remaining is to be stoned to death."

SHORT-TERM COMMITMENT

Another day in the chai shop, Mali asked Nasruddin, "Why is it that you never speak your wife's name?"

"It's simple. Because I have no idea what it is," said the Mullah.

"What? How long have you been married?"

"Let me think," Mullah said, scratching his beard. "I think we've been married now maybe twenty years, give or take a few."

Mali asked, "Mullah, that's incredible. You're married now for two decades, and you don't know your wife's name?"

"Way back then, when we were wed, by our parents' arrangement, I had no intention of making a go at the marriage, so why should I have bothered to learn her name?"

"It's Fatima, you dolt. You really can't remember the year you married Fatima, your wife of more than twenty years?"

"To tell the truth, I don't remember exactly when we got married," Nasruddin replied. "As should be clear to you by now, it happened long before I had any sense whatsoever."

THE BENEFICENT PLACE

When Fatima died, Nasruddin sat down beside her body and wept pitifully, with his head buried between his wife's thighs.

Fatima's friend Setare quietly suggested to him, "Sit down, and weep, by all means — but better to cry at her head!"

Nasruddin could only manage to sob, "But I'm putting my tears in the place that has benefited me the most!"

CHECK AND MATE

Nasruddin liked to play chess with his old friends at the chai shop, and often he and the other chess players gave one another hints and tips as they watched each other play.

Over time, however, the Mullah's unrequested guidance became so bothersome that his friends made him vow to divorce his wife if he would ever intervene again in another's game with advice.

A few days later, Nasruddin went to the chai shop, where Ali and Mesut were in the midst of a chess match. He stepped closer and observed the game. Almost immediately, he saw that Faik needed to make a crucial move to win the game.

At first, he struggled to remain silent, but after a few moments the Mullah couldn't resist kibbitzing. He burst out saying, "Do you not see what you must do, Faik? You should move your queen up and take the rook."

"Mullah," said Ali, obviously annoyed, "did you not promise to separate from your wife, if you ever interrupted us at chess again?"

Mullah said, "I offer my advice only in jest. In fact, I even got married as a joke."

Faik snarled, "Well, go away from here and leave us alone. It's not funny, and it's not appreciated."

"Go ahead and make your move already," urged Nasruddin, heading for the door, "and I'll go and renew my marriage vows."

OPEN SESAME

Fatima and Kerima, Nasruddin's two wives, came to him together. "Husband, we are confused and need your guidance," Kerima confessed.

Nasruddin asked, "What is the problem?"

Fatima confessed, "We have made a mistake," said Fatima, "both of us have pissed into a jar in a dark corner."

"And so what is the issue, exactly?"

Kerima answered, "One of us has passed urine, and the other peed sesame oil. But we cannot tell who of us has done what in which jar."

"This is easy to find out," exclaimed the Mullah. "Lie face down on the ground, and let me stamp on your asses. Then we'll know: whichever of you yields crushed sesame seeds is the one who produced the oil."

SEEING DOUBLE

Some months after the death of Fatima, the Mullah's neighbors Hussein and Setare encouraged him to court and marry Setare's younger cousin, Kerima, who was an attractive, sweet-natured woman with a roving left eye, which made her see double. "Her eyes are beguiling," they claimed, "and fascinating beyond description."

Mullah resisted the idea at first, but eventually, after some prodding, he agreed to marry her.

One night soon after they wed, Mullah brought her a dish of ice cream to share.

"Are we expecting company?" asked Kerima. "One dish would have been sufficient, but two dishes — it's a bit extravagant, is it not?"

"In our house," Nasruddin assured his new wife, "it is perfectly all right to see anything double, especially when it is food."

They laughed, and were just beginning to eat the ice cream when she sat upright and whispered, "Pardon me, dear husband, but you are surely mistaken if you take me for a woman with no sense of propriety."

"Whatever do you mean?"

"Tell me — who is that man there, the Mullah sitting right next to you?"

"Damn you, woman!" cursed Nasruddin, jumping up from the table. "It's fine to see anything in duplicate, except when you are looking at your husband!

THE SPRINTER

Shortly after Nasruddin had become a widower, he married again and, after a mere three months, his young wife, Kerima, bore him a son.

When Kerima's mother, Meryem, and her other relatives came to see the baby, they disagreed and started to argue about the child's name.

Suddenly, Nasruddin stood up and announced, "I have already made my decision and chosen a name. My boy will be called Sprinter."

"But that's not a proper name for a child," Meryem objected, "that's like a name for . . . a horse."

"True, but the kid has galloped through a journey of nine months in only three months. If anyone deserves the right to be called Sprinter, it's him."

DO THE MATH

Just three months after Nasruddin married Kerima, she gave birth to a boy. Confused about the early arrival, he asked, "How did that happen so fast?"

She said, "You see, it's all very straightforward. There is a very simple explanation for that. It has been three months since I married you, right?"

Nasruddin slowly nodded his agreement.

"So, there's three months," continued Kerima. "That's ninety days. Plus three more months since you married me, which makes six months." Mullah agreed.

"And you said that the baby came in three months. So that makes nine months altogether, correct?"

Nasruddin scratched his beard and replied, "I guess . . . math was never my strong suit. You must be right, my dear."

JOY OR JUNK

One day, when Nasruddin's young wife Kerima thought nobody was in the house, she undressed and sat on a chair with a small hand mirror, admiring her vagina.

As she looked at her pussy this way and that, she exclaimed, "Oh, my darling! My precious delight! Why did I not possess three of your sort? You are my joy and my satisfaction. How much happiness I have experienced because of you! And who knows how much good fortune I will have in the future due to your grace?"

The Mullah happened to be passing outside her window on his way to the garden and heard every word of her self-praise. So he went to the garden, pulled out his cock and balls, and yelled, "Damn you, fiendish tube of hairy flesh! You motherfucking devil, with your two demented boys! It's all because of you that I have so much trouble and misfortune. And Allah alone knows how much misery you will bring me yet!"

His wife heard him inside the house. She looked out the window and saw the Mullah standing outside in the garden ranting at his exposed penis and scrotum.

Fatima exclaimed, "Mullah! What's your problem?"

The Mullah shouted, "Don't disturb me, you conceited bitch! I didn't bother you while you were rejoicing your cunt. Why do you interrupt me while I am mourning my junk? How unfair is it, that in the same place where a woman thinks she has a divine treasure, we men are led to believe that what we possess between our legs is an endless source of evil and suffering?"

PART IV

Meet the Nasruddins

Boys like nuts

One day, Nasruddin came home just as his wife Fatima was about to give birth. He asked, "What are all these people doing here?"

Setare, the midwife, told the Mullah, "Just go away and take a little walk." So Nasruddin went out for a long, pleasant stroll through the village.

When he returned home, again they told him, "Go away just a bit longer."

So the Mullah took another stroll, and after a while, he returned home. But when once again they told Nasruddin to leave, he began to berate and throw out all the people. Then he went to his wife's side and rolled some walnuts from her stomach to her vagina. She asked, "Mullah! What are you doing?"

He replied, "You, whom I have fucked! What else am I supposed to do? It's a boy, and all boys like nuts. I thought that I could entice him out with nuts."

Whoever sees the light

When Mullah Nasruddin's wife, Fatima, was pregnant for the first time, she went into labor early in the evening, attended carefully in the bedroom by their neighbor Setare, the midwife, while Nasruddin nervously waited outside. Many hours passed before anything happened. Though he tried to stay awake, Nasruddin was ready to fall asleep standing up when finally, just as dawn's early light appeared on the eastern horizon, Setare came out and said, "Congratulations, Nasruddin. It's a healthy baby boy!"

As the midwife returned to Fatima's side, Nasruddin could see the sun rising through the bedroom window. Nasruddin was beside himself with pride, and he rushed to tell the neighbors.

"Congratulate me! I have just had a child."

"Marvelous, Nasruddin! Is it a boy or a girl?" said Hussein.

"Yes — how did you know?"

Nasruddin returned to wait outside the bedroom. After a few minutes, Setare called out to him again, exclaiming, "Well done, Nasruddin! You also have a girl!"

As the midwife returned to the bedroom, Nasruddin could see the sun rising over the horizon. He was undoubtedly still proud, but now he started to wonder how would he feed two more mouths on his meager income as a young mullah.

Nasruddin stepped back outside to consult Hussein. "Congratulate me! I have just had another child."

"Wonderful, Nasruddin. Is it a girl or a boy?"

"Yes — but how in the world could you have possibly known?"

They were interrupted by Setare, who stuck her head out the door and called to Nasruddin, "Brace yourself, Nasruddin — it's twin girls."

Nasruddin suddenly rushed into the bedroom, grabbed the quilt and bedcovers off Fatima, threw the bedding over the window, and blew out the room lamps.

Fatima shrieked, "Nasruddin, what are you doing?"

"What else can I do?" he cried, "Whoever sees the light wants to come out."

LOCATION IS EVERYTHING

Eventually, a son was born to Nasruddin and Fatima, and Setare the midwife requested him to participate. "Please, Mullah, since you have a blessed hand," she praised him, "you should cut the umbilical cord."

The Mullah replied, "Gladly."

He grabbed the baby's umbilical cord and yanked it until he ripped it out. As this left a hole, Setare screamed at him, "Mullah, what have you done?"

Nasruddin answered calmly, "If it doesn't make all that much difference, then he can just have his asshole placed right here."

STUCK IN THE MUD

One day, Nasruddin came home and said to Fatima, "My dear, why don't you cook a nice pilaf? I feel very good today. Let's have a nice evening."

Fatima made a lovely pilaf for supper, which they enjoyed much. After they cleaned up and were getting ready for bed, there was a knock at the door. Fatima answered it and discovered her neighbor, Setare, standing there, anxious to gossip about the news of the day.

"Our donkey had twins this morning," shared Setare, walking right in. "One of the little ones is perfectly normal. But the other one was born without a tail or ears. It seems so peculiar." The women chatted briefly about this and that, and eventually, the neighbor left.

When Fatima returned to bed, Nasruddin asked, "So what's up with our neighbors, Setare and Hussein?"

Fatima replied, "Oh, don't even ask. Their jenny-mule had twins this morning, but one of the little donkeys was born without a tail or ears. How weird."

Hearing this, the Mullah became enraged, growling, "Oh, that's just fucking lovely. Maybe twice a year, we decide to have a pleasant evening together — and then the neighbor's donkey gives birth to twins, and it's all ruined!"

"Mullah, calm down," said Fatima, "it's hardly of any consequence. Why should you get all bent out of shape about the neighbor's deformed baby donkey?"

Nasruddin fumed, "Is it possible *not* to be upset about such a thing? Think about this for a minute. Three years from now, the animal will be three years old. It'll be taken by Hussein to the mountain to haul firewood, and one day the animal will likely get stuck in the mud of a swamp, and he won't be able to move it. So naturally, Hussein will appeal to me for help, and then since the donkey won't have ears or a tail, there will be nothing at all to hold on to, to pull it out of the mud. What a dire predicament we'll no doubt find ourselves in then"

SOMETHING TO PLAY WITH

One day, Fatima handed the baby to Nasruddin and said to him, "I have to go fetch water. Keep the boy calm until I come back! If he fusses, simply give the child something to play with."

She went to the well, but once she was gone, the baby began to cry. Nasruddin knew nothing better to do than give the child his dick in his hand to play with.

When his wife came back and saw the baby playing happily with Nasruddin's erect cock, she exclaimed, "You brainless idiot! What do you think you are doing?"

"You, whom I have fucked!" shouted the Mullah. "You told me to give the little devil something to play with if he cried. Should I have given him a knife with which he would cut his hand and bleed to death?"

A SEPARATE EXISTENCE

Once, Nasruddin and Fatima had quarreled bitterly in their bedroom, with their infant sleeping peaceably in his crib.

The argument escalated until it almost came to blows. Then the Mullah suddenly grabbed the cradle with the child and slid it between her bed and his. He spoke to the child, "There! Now your mother and I are officially separated. Kindly inform her that I hereby disown her from my presence."

SLEEPING AID

Fatima came to Nasruddin one night holding their child and said, "Mullah, please help: I don't know what the matter is with our baby boy. Ahmet won't stop crying, and nothing I can do will make him quiet. Would you write a spell or recite a little prayer from some holy book? Do whatever you want to. My arms are exhausted from carrying and rocking him night and day."

Nasruddin replied, "My dear, do not worry. Just take this scholarly religious text, place it in front of the kid, and turn the pages once in a while."

"Dolt! Are you making fun of me? The child cannot read. How do you think this book will make the baby sleep?"

Mullah said, "Listen to me, bitch — this book is very thick and dense. Whenever I take it out and begin teaching it to the students at the madrasa, they all always immediately start yawning and become very drowsy. If the book can make smart young men fall asleep, surely it will make this stupid kid nod off."

PUTTING OUT ROOTS

Once Nasruddin observed a grove of trees and thought, *Since those trees bear fruit, why shouldn't I?*

So Mullah went to the field and buried himself up to his belly in the ground. When night fell, he became cold, and so he dug himself out and returned home.

The next day, when Fatima asked him how it went, he said, "It was okay at first. I was just about to put out roots when the cold started to kill them."

GETTING BABY TO SLEEP

When Fatima had to go to the well one morning, she put the child in Nasruddin's lap and told him, "Keep the boy calm until I come back."

She went, but as soon as she was gone, the baby began fussing. The Mullah did not know what to do. Then he remembered that they had yogurt in an earthen jar in the kitchen, but he couldn't find a spoon. So he rubbed some curds on his dick and let the baby lick it off until he went to sleep.

When his wife came home, she cried, "Well, Nasruddin! How beautiful you look with the baby asleep in your arms."

"You lousy cunt," said the Mullah. "I had to feed him nine lots of yogurt with my cock until at last he finally fell asleep. If only I could feed you that way so that you would fall asleep!"

PISSING MATCH

One day, Fatima handed the baby to Nasruddin and said, "I have to run out to borrow a little salt from the neighbor. Keep Ahmet calm until I come back."

After Fatima left, the boy was peaceable for a while. Eventually, though, the baby began to fuss. So Nasruddin took Ahmet and bounced him gently on his knee for several minutes. But instead of calming the boy, the child peed on him.

So Nasruddin sat the kid on the floor, stood up, and shat on him.

A minute later, when Fatima came back and saw what he had done, she screamed at Nasruddin, "You fool! What have you done?"

"You, whom I have fucked!" Nasruddin yelled back. "Do you really think that I'm about to let the little bastard have the last word? You're daft if you think I'm about to give him the upper hand."

TOO MUCH PROSPERITY

Mullah Nasruddin had taught his son, Ahmet, that, every time he sneezed, he should clap his hands and shout, "God be praised!" with the inner meaning of: "May you prosper, Father."

One day he dropped the bucket into the well, and Nasruddin asked Ahmet to climb down and get it out. But he was afraid and refused to obey him. So the Mullah undressed, tied a rope around his waist, and lowered himself slowly into the well.

Once the Mullah grabbed the bucket, Ahmet began to pull him back up but, just as he was almost to the top of the well, he sneezed. Ahmet, obediently following his father's instructions, released the rope to clap his hands and merrily chant, "God be praised, Father fell!" which dunked Nasruddin back in the well and injured him while falling.

When he finally climbed out of the well, he collapsed on the ground, groaning in pain and observed, "Do not fear, my boy, it was not your fault but mine. Too much prosperity a man can never have."

SHOULDERED BOY

One day when the Mullah went to market, he carried his young son on his shoulders. He was going along pleasantly enough when he suddenly thought, *I have lost Ahmet, my child!* So he began frantically running around the market looking for him.

He searched and searched for a long time but, at long last, he gave up and decided to head back home. On the way, he passed a halvah shop, and Ahmet called out atop from the Mullah's shoulders, "Father, I'm hungry. Would you please buy me a bit of halvah here?"

"Ah, there you are, you son of a bastard!" shouted the Mullah at his long-lost son. "I couldn't find you anywhere. Why didn't you speak up earlier? I've been looking for you all morning long."

EGGS OR BALLS

A year after giving birth to a healthy son, Fatima gave birth to a daughter, Hafiza, and because she wanted another boy she told her husband, "Oh Nasruddin! How I wish she had two balls between her legs."

The Mullah said, "Don't worry, my dear. Our daughter is a jewel. Just pray to Allah that she lives a long and healthy life — no doubt, when she's grown up, she will find plenty of balls abiding there."

EXPLAINING AN EGGPLANT

One day, Hamza brought Mullah Nasruddin a small eggplant, saying, "Mullah, I wonder what this might be. Please tell me."

He took the object and turned it around and over in his hands, examining the odd purplish thing. After several minutes of this inspection, he said, "Hamza, my friend, I cannot tell you. But let us take it to my son, Ahmet. He will know better than me."

They took the eggplant to Ahmet and showed it to him. He examined it before finally declaring, "You ridiculous old farts. What's so hard about figuring it out? Obviously, this is a baby starling whose eyes have not yet opened."

WHITE HALVAH

Nasruddin was walking in the market with his son, Ahmet, when he pointed to a white halvah and asked, "Boy, do you know what that is?"

Ahmet answered, "That is a pot with white onions."

Mullah said, "If I taught that to God, surely He would deny me His grace."

KNUCKLEBONE

Nasruddin went to the market with his boy when he purchased some liver for dinner. Ahmet said, "Father, please give me the small knucklebones out of the liver."

The Mullah yelled, "Son of a bitch! Do you really think that the liver has a knucklebone?" And Nasruddin punched the boy, which sent the child running in tears all the way home.

When the Mullah arrived home, Fatima scolded him, "May the Devil take you! What did the boy do to make you hit him and send him home crying in pain?"

The Mullah said, "The little bastard wanted a knucklebone in the liver. So I gave him one."

"How should the poor child know better than that?" replied Fatima. "He thought it was tripe in your hand."

TWO HANDSFUL OF BARLEY

Nasruddin grew a field of barley that was still green, and for some odd reason the previous year, it was always being trampled down in spots. This year, however, after much work and vigilance, Nasruddin's grain was looking very fine.

Nasruddin's daughter, Hafiza, had a well-built lover, Yılmaz, who liked to take her in the tall grass. Once he came to her and said, "Hey, let's get it on! I will be the stallion, and you will be the mare."

Hafiza agreed and took him out back to the field. Yılmaz chose a spot in the middle, and they got down to business. While she was riding her mount, she grabbed a bunch of barley in each hand to playfully whip his long, lean torso.

After a minute of hard riding, Yılmaz noticed that Mullah was standing at the edge of the field, watching them silently. Quickly he bucked his rider off of him, jumped into his pants and sandals, and her stallion galloped away.

Hafiza, still naked but unaware her father was nearby, jumped up and chased after her lover, yelling, "Whoa, big fella! My stallion, where are you running so fast? Whoa!" while waving the stalks of grain at him.

"Daughter, thank you for solving the mystery," called out the Mullah, "but do you honestly expect a cocksman like him, who abandons a pussy as lovely as yours, to return for a measly two handsful of barley?"

THE UNCUT MELON

Once Nasruddin's wife asked him not to send his teenage daughter on errands around town. "I am afraid for Hafiza's safety and chastity," Fatima declared, "since she is an uncut melon," referring to her daughter's virginity.

That evening, the family was sitting together in the living room when the girl's dress slipped open and parted. The Mullah noticed his daughter's bare vulva exposed and remarked to his wife, "Fatima! You said that this is an uncut melon, but I can clearly see that it has been cloven. It most certainly has become two pieces."

Upon hearing this, Fatima scolded her daughter, "My dear! Cover your *poça*," using an old Persian word that means both "the end of the spinal cord" (perineum) and "useless."

The Mullah said, "Fatima, my dear, just wait until we find our lovely Hafiza a suitor! Rather than being *poça*, it will become something quite useful."

The Silent Treatment

Nasruddin was tired of feeding and washing his donkey, so he asked his wife Fatima to do it. She refused, and the argument rose to the level of a dispute in which they decided that whoever speaks first should feed the donkey.

For a while, Nasruddin sat stoically in a corner and sulked. Fatima soon became quite bored and left with their son Ahmet to visit the neighbors.

Now, that day there happened to be a family of Gypsies who had pitched their camp outside the town, and they wandered around town, looking hither and thither to find something to steal.

One of them entered the house of Nasruddin, where it was silent. In the family quarters, she saw the Mullah, but he remained sitting impassively in the corner. Immediately she called the rest of the Gypsies, and they ransacked the house, grabbed everything they could find together, and placed it in their bags.

The Mullah sat in his corner and witnessed this entire debacle as it proceeded without moving or saying a word. The head Gypsy even snatched the turban off his head, but he never uttered a word, thinking, *If I make a sound, then Fatima will win, and I will be obliged to feed and water and wash the calf!* So he did not even heed to the Gypsy, who exploited his passivity. When the band of thieves had looted enough, they left the house with the front door wide open.

At dinnertime, Fatima was still enjoying herself, gossiping nonstop with the neighbors, and she sent Ahmet with a bowl of soup to bring to Nasruddin.

Ahmet was understandably confused when he got home to see the front door left open. Inside, he found his father there sitting in the corner alone with the place in shambles.

Ahmet cried out, "Father, what happened?" Nasruddin kept pointing to his head to indicate his stolen turban, but the boy misinterpreted the strange gestures and emptied the bowl of soup on Nasruddin's head, then beat a hasty retreat to inform his mother what happened.

When Fatima learned of the situation from Ahmet, they rushed back, she saw the house ransacked, all the drawers and doors open, the valuables gone, Nasruddin sitting in the corner, silent but scowling, covered with soup.

"What have you done, you brain-dead fool?" she shrieked. "Where's our furniture? What the—?"

"Ha ha ha, now you must feed and wash the donkey," Nasruddin said with glee, jumping up and clapping. "And I hope you're pleased with what you accomplished through your boneheaded stubbornness."

DON'T GO ANYWHERE

One day, Mullah Nasruddin was sitting at the chai shop when Sedat rushed in and told him, "Your son, Ahmet, had fallen into our well. Please come now to rescue him!"

Nasruddin rushed to the well and called, "Ahmet! Are you still there?"

Ahmet cried out in despair from the bottom of the well, "Yes, Father, I am here, and I'm freezing! Please, please help me!"

Nasruddin replied, "Okay, son, everything's under control. I'll run home and bring a rope to pull you out. But listen carefully: you mustn't go wandering off anywhere. Stay right where you are — and I'll be right back."

WHAT THE BOY LOST

One day, Nasruddin's son went to the hammam. After several hours, Mesut the hammamji came to Mullah's house and told him, "Today at the hammam, your moronic son Ahmet lost his mind."

Mullah responded, "Forget it — you must be mistaking my Ahmet for someone else. You see, the boy has lost his mind already, a long time ago. So while he was at the hammam, he must have lost something else."

DOUBLE THE DOWRY

Having failed on his own to sell his cow at the bazaar, Mullah Nasruddin gave the animal to an auctioneer, who managed to convince some fool to buy the cow at market price because it was both a virgin and six months pregnant.

Meanwhile, Nasruddin had a comely daughter, Hafiza, who had come of age, so a few women from neighboring towns came to consider her potential as an arranged bride for their sons.

Everything went well between the family and the ladies during the interview, when Nasruddin blurted out, "The girl's pregnant — but just a little bit so."

After a moment of stunned silence, Hafiza covered her face and ran from the room in shame, and the mothers stood up and left. Then Fatima scolded him,

"You witless shithead! Everyone in the region will hear of this by morning! Now you have utterly ruined all possibility of arranging her marriage!"

"You brainless twit," said the Mullah. "If you sell a cow or horse on the market and say that it is pregnant, rather than complain, people will pay even more money! Why shouldn't I expect the same results with our daughter?"

A WORTHY FLOWER

As Mullah Nasruddin prepared to make love to Fatima, by chance a honeybee flew in the window and landed on the head of his erection.

As the yellow-black insect danced all around his engorged glans head, he declared with glee to the bee, "My friend, this goes to show that you know what's good! You have indeed selected a blooming purple flower ready and worthy for nectar preparation!"

TELL THE TRUTH

Fatima was in the habit of going out every evening to gossip, play cards, and have fun with the neighbors, often not returning until early in the morning.

Finally, one night, Nasruddin got fed up, and he locked and bolted the door against his wife. When Fatima came home, she begged and pleaded with the Mullah to let her in, but he pretended to be deaf to her screams.

"If you don't let me in, I'm going to throw myself in the garden well and drown!"

"Be my guest, you fucking whore," replied Nasruddin.

Fatima went to the backyard and found a large stone. Hauling the rock to the well, she managed to throw it in, which made a loud kerplunk. Then she ran and hid around the corner of the house.

Nasruddin, hearing the splash, believed Fatima to have jumped in the well, so he rushed out the back door in his nightgown. As he peered into the dark well, trying to discern if his wife was still alive, Fatima crept silently into the house. She banged the door shut and locked it securely against her enraged husband.

When Nasruddin heard the door slam behind him, he realized his wife had gotten the upper hand. He pounded the door, but Fatima answered with a strong of insults, "You filthy swine, you unfaithful husband, you miserable donkeyfucker!

You come home late each night after cavorting around with skanky whores and filthy men!"

As usual, nosy neighbors are not far away, and so Hussein came out to see what was causing the commotion. He asked, "What's the problem, Mullah?"

Nasruddin, rendered almost speechless, could only mutter, "My friend, I do not know of all the sins of which I am accused. But I know that those who comprehend the truth should speak out, for the sake of Allah."

HANDS WERE FULL

When Nasruddin went on a long trip, Fatima insisted that he carry a weapon, so he left heavily armed. In one hand, he held a huge sword, and in the other, he clenched a pistol. Unfortunately, on the road, the Mullah encountered a thief who stopped and robbed him. Not even the Mullah's pants were left him.

When he returned home and told Fatima what had happened to him, she exclaimed, "You dolt. You were armed to the teeth! Why in God's name did you not do anything to defend yourself?"

Nasruddin defended himself, "How could I? I had my hands full. If I had had my hands free, I would have strangled him. But eventually, I gave him a scare as bad as the fright he gave me."

"How did you manage to do that?" asked Fatima.

"Well, after he'd gone about half a mile, I yelled the nastiest, fiercest insults at him. There wasn't a curse word known to man that I didn't use to threaten him. I'm sure that his ears are still burning."

SO CLEVER

One day, Nasruddin's son, Ahmet, said to him, "Father, I can still remember when you were born."

Fatima became quite troubled by Ahmet's statement and cried, "What does the boy mean by this nonsense? What a strange thing to say, the son of a bitch."

Nasruddin calmly replied, "Oh, Fatima, do not be angry. What does it matter? The boy is so clever that it is quite possible that he actually knows what he's talking about."

PREVENTIVE MEASURE

M ullah Nasruddin woke up one morning, yawned, and decided that he would bathe early. He needed water for his bath but discovered there was none, so he called for his six-year-old son, Ahmet, to fetch some. He handed him a sizable ceramic vase and told him to go fill the container at the nearby well.

Ahmet took the vessel and turned, ready to go, but then Nasruddin swatted him across the back and yelled, "And don't break it!" which made the lad stumble forward, nearly dropping the fragile vessel.

Fatima, who had watched this whole vase-and-punishment episode, reproached Nasruddin. "Mullah, why were you so harsh with Ahmet? Why did you punish him before he had broken anything or done something wrong?"

Nasruddin lowered his eyebrows and regarded her indignantly. "Don't be foolish. It wouldn't do any good to reprimand him after he broke the vase, would it?"

WORTHY OF THE FINEST CREAM

O ne morning, Fatima sent Ahmet, her son, out to the market to buy milk.

The Shah happened to be in the town square and, noticing Nasruddin's boy rush by with the empty milk bottle, decided to have some fun. He called out, "Boy! Stop and tell me, where in the world are you running so fast?"

"I have to go to the market to buy milk."

"Nonsense, boy, come here," the Shah beckoned Ahmet to his side. "Why should you buy what is available for free? Give your bottle to me and wait here. I will have my guards fill it with sweet milk for you." So the Shah took the boy's bottle and ordered the guards to fill it with their spit and semen, which they quickly accomplished as he watched with hilarity. When it was over, the Shah returned to Ahmet and handed the bottle filled with the milky-white fluid back to the boy and sent him on his way.

When Ahmet and his mother revealed to Nasruddin everything about the Shah's nasty prank, the Mullah decided to return the favor. He waited a few days until he heard that the Shah had been suffering from migraines, then scooped up some horseshit, pissed and ejaculated into the pail, and stirred it around until it was the consistency of frothy paste. Then he poured the Santorum-like mixture into a jug and hurried to the palace.

"Your Majesty," Nasruddin addressed the Shah, who was holding his head in pain, in a soft, gentle tone. "I have brought you a strong but soothing poultice that will most certainly bring you relief from your infernal headaches. The aged and wise healer who gave it to me — may Allah bless her soul — directed that it be applied generously to the scalp and neck three times a day. She recommended that you not wash the area between applications. It is said to banish even the most horrific pain."

The Shah was willing to try anything at this point, and so he took the jug with the dark-looking ointment and applied the salve as Nasruddin instructed. On the third day, however, he found no relief from his migraines and could no longer stand the stench and insects the poultice attracted. He had his underlings fetch Nasruddin.

When the Mullah appeared at the Shah's bedside, he said, "Yes, Majesty, how may I be of service?"

"Tell me, Nasruddin, what is this atrocious remedy made of?" asked the Shah.

"Usually it is made of milk," the Mullah answered, "but naturally I would consider your Majesty worthy only of the finest cream."

SAME AS HE EVER WAS

One day, Mullah Nasruddin jumped over a brook. As he leaped, he broke wind and trumped loudly. He laughed and sighed, "Ah, youth!"

Ahmet, his son, was passing by and heard his father's long fart. He called out to Nasruddin, "Even in your youth, Father, you must have been quite a pig."

WHOM ELSE TO ASK?

When they were both adults, Mullah Nasruddin asked his older brother, "Please, Selim, at long last, do me a huge favor."

"What can I do for you?"

"Let me take you as I used to when you were as a young boy."

"No! Can't you ask me to do anything else?" protested Selim.

"Well, why not?" said the Mullah. "You're my brother. Whom else am I supposed to ask?"

SWEET MEDICINE

Once, Nasruddin's aged mother, Leyla, took ill and so he brought his ailing mother to the town physician, Hamid. After he thoroughly examined Leyla, the doctor then made the diagnosis that the elderly woman needed a man to mount her and provide internal stimulation to rejuvenate her.

"How can I find someone who is qualified to do this therapy?" asked the Mullah.

Hamid responded, "It's not my usual practice, but I am qualified to administer such treatment and act as a husband to her." Nasruddin was skeptical but agreed.

As the physician was applying the cure to Leyla's malady, Nasruddin said, "Hamid must be the wisest of physicians to know such a sweet medicine."

THE EGG TREE

When Mullah Nasruddin and his son, Ahmet, were walking with Jalal, they came to an apricot tree. Jalal stopped and asked the boy, "Tell us, boy, do you know what kind of tree is this?"

Ahmet contemplated the matter for a minute, and replied, "At first, I think, it was an egg tree. At some point, though, rain and hail must have fallen from the sky, broken the eggshells, and washed away the egg whites, so that now only the yolks remain clinging to the tree."

Nasruddin said to Jalal, "The little bastard, how did he figure that one out all by himself? I swear, I didn't teach it to him."

ONLY PROPER

Nasruddin was riding on his donkey, Karakacan, along a remote road when he got horny. So he dismounted near a large tree, got behind the animal, and fucked the beast with gusto.

After a rather lengthy session, he relaxed, sitting with his back against the tree trunk, with his long cock hanging out, drying in the sun. Before long, the Mullah had nodded off for a nap.

Hamid, the village doctor, happened to walk by on that road and saw Nasruddin drowsing with his junk exposed. He kicked the Mullah and shouted, "What are you doing? By my Willie! What a fucking disgrace! Hide your shame."

Nasruddin only replied, "Leave me alone, you whose accursed tribe I fuck! You think I should cover my pecker while it's still wet so that it gets all moldy? Why shouldn't I let it dry off? In truth, it's only the proper thing to do before I go home and use it with my wife."

THE FAMILY OF STRANGERS

Mullah Nasruddin approached and told his sister, Hayat, "You should give me something once and for all."

Hayat replied, "Tell me: what should I give to you, brother?"

Nasruddin answered, "I would like it very much if you would give me whatever it is that you give to the boys in the neighborhood."

Hayat said, "Forget it! I'm your sister. Why don't you ask for that from some stranger, instead of me?"

He answered indignantly, "Well, you won't give me some, even though you're my sister. When my own family refuses my simple requests, then why do you think that some stranger would ever want to give it to me?"

FINAL INSTRUCTION

When the Mullah had sent his daughter, Hafiza, to another village to be wed, some local married women came to the house to escort her to her new home.

They were miles on their way when they heard the Mullah yelling from behind. He had run all the way to catch up with the bridal procession, and everyone was surprised to see him. He clasped his daughter's hands in his and breathlessly said, "My darling girl Hafiza, I almost forgot to give you my final instruction."

"Yes, dear Father," she said, "what is it?"

"Bear in mind that, when you sew, you should always make a knot at the end of the thread before you pass the other end through the eye of the needle. Don't ever forget that."

MAKING A RACKET

One day, Kerima asked her husband, "Mullah, why do you not fart after you piss, like other men?" He had no answer to that, so he said nothing.

The next day, while he was taking his morning pee, he remembered what his wife had said, and he let out a loud, lengthy fart. A guy passing outside heard the trumping and yelled, "By my Willie! What a racket!"

Nasruddin yelled back, "Hey, you nosy son of an ass! Go plug your Willie into the whore who taught me that trick!"

TIT FOR TAT

One day, the Mullah's married daughter, Hafiza, came home with her head in her hands, crying pitifully. When Nasruddin asked her to tell him her problem, the girl revealed a black right eye. She appealed to her father for consolation and support, crying, "I am an abused wife. My husband has lost his mind. In front of the child, the madman cursed and assaulted me."

In response, the Mullah slapped his daughter on the other cheek, saying, "Go back to your lousy husband and tell the bastard that the Mullah is no man's fool. If that no-good prick is going to abuse my daughter, he can rest assured that in retaliation, I will beat his wife."

THE DONKEY EGG

From a brown leather sack, Hamza brought forth a large, smooth, golden-orange, oval object. He held it out in offering to the Nasruddins, smiling broadly, as he stood before them in front of their house.

"It's a donkey egg," Hamza explained, before handing it to Fatima. It felt solid and hefty, like a rock. "Just sit on the egg — very gently — for no more than three weeks. Then a baby donkey will hatch from the egg, and in a few months you'll have a second sturdy donkey to carry your loads."

"With two donkeys, we could even take a trip together," suggested Nasruddin to Fatima. The couple was amazed at Hamza's unexpected generosity. They never had before thought of him a being a good neighbor. Why, just last week, Nasruddin had quarreled with Hamza at the chai shop about some trivial matter. And now, here he was, showing up at their house with a gift.

"We are blessed by your kindness," said Nasruddin, "and grateful for your friendship."

After Hamza departed, they got right to work. The next three weeks were long ones for the Nasruddins. While the Mullah sat ever so lightly on the donkey egg, Fatima cleaned house, prepared the meals, and visited the neighbor women. While Fatima crouched over the egg, Nasruddin chopped wood, went to market, and sat around the chai shop with his friends.

When friends asked if they could see the donkey egg, they refused, saying, "Sorry, but we can't take the chance of letting it get cold, not even for a moment."

After three weeks, they noticed the donkey egg had gotten much softer, but showed no sign of swelling or producing a baby. After three more excruciatingly slow days, the egg was quite squishy to the touch and started to smell funny.

Finally, the Nasruddins decided that they had had quite enough of the donkey egg that seemed unlikely ever to bring them a little animal. Sadly, the Mullah wrapped the withered thing in a sack and carried it out of the village. In his sorrow, he couldn't understand why some of the village children ran behind him laughing and chanting, "Donkey eggs come from pumpkin vines! Donkey eggs come from pumpkin vines!"

At the top of a verdant hill, Nasruddin opened the bag and let the doomed donkey egg plop out. It rolled down the hillside, picking up speed until it passed a walnut tree where a rabbit was napping peacefully and smashed against another large rock. The sound frightened the sleeping bunny, which jumped up and ran uphill past the Mullah, who was too astounded to move to catch the critter.

"I cannot believe it," cried the exasperated Nasruddin. "After waiting for so many weeks, the donkey egg was at last ready to hatch. Now our baby donkey is lost forever. If only we'd had a little more patience. May Allah save me!"

PART V
Donkey Tales
&
Animal Crackers

DECREE FOR A DONKEY

Karakacan, Mullah Nasruddin's little gray donkey, became fed up with carrying heavy loads, always being cursed verbally, and receiving regular whippings, as well as all sorts of other abuse, so she went to court to petition to get her freedom from her owner. She detailed her poor treatment at the hands of the Mullah, and the judge issued a decree stating that the creature was freed from being an indentured donkey.

When Karakacan brought back the decree to Nasruddin and showed him that she was no longer obligated to act as a servant or slave, he was furious. He tore the document into a hundred pieces and put the shredded paper into Karakacan's feedbag. Naturally, the donkey could not help but to inadvertently eat it, the next day dropping it in a pile on the road as she trudged along with the Mullah on her back, no longer a free donkey.

That is why it is said that all donkeys walking along any road are compelled to stop every time they encounter a pile of donkey dung and sniff it. They are merely hoping that, someday, somehow, they will detect the remains of the decree issued to the Mullah's little gray donkey that set her free.

WOLVES THAT EAT NO SHEEP

Once Nasruddin was traveling and encountered an old shepherd who told him, "I have already raised many sheep, but too many of them have been killed and devoured by wolves. Mullah, what is your opinion: are there any wolves in this world that do not eat sheep?"

"Of course," answered Nasruddin.

"And where are they? Tell me at once!"

"Dead," replied Nasruddin.

THE MAN FROM HOMS

Once while on pilgrimage, Mullah Nasruddin was riding his donkey at a steady pace down a narrow lane when he came up behind another fellow, riding a much slower mule. So he shouted to the chap, "Get out of my way, you man from Homs!"

Homs, as you may know, is a city located in western Syria. The mule rider turned around and replied in astonishment to Nasruddin, "How in Allah's name did you know that I am from Homs?"

The Mullah replied, "As I approached you from behind I noticed that the vagina of your mule looks like the Arabic letter *h*; I saw the anus, which resembles the letter *m*; and I saw the tail, which is similar to the letter *s*. Then I figured it out: This fellow must have come from Homs!"

ACCEPT AND ADJUST

While walking near Lake Akşehir one morning, Mullah Nasruddin encountered a huge turtle. Seeing the Mullah, the turtle tried to beat a hasty retreat. However, Nasruddin noticed how agilely the creature moved and exclaimed, "What a strong and sturdy steed you would be for me if only such an ugly and wild beast such as you could be tamed!"

Acting decisively, he leaped at the turtle, seized its shell and sat down on its back. The turtle, however, struggled mightily to throw him off.

Nasruddin yelled, "You can shake all you want in a vain attempt to dislodge me, but mark my words: sooner or later, you'll get accustomed to carrying your new master!"

A MATTER OF BREEDING

One day in the chai shop, Mullah Nasruddin met a very dignified junior diplomat traveling through town. The two enjoyed some conversation together before parting company. As Nasruddin boarded his old donkey, he said, "Goodbye, my messenger friend! It was a pleasure meeting such a fine young agent."

The fellow bristled at the insult. "Mullah! Kindly refrain from addressing me as a messenger or agent; rather, say: 'Your Emissary.'"

"Why?" asked Nasruddin.

"I have an excellent reason for calling myself neither a messenger nor an agent, thank you very much. Primarily because of my royal pedigree. My brother and I are both official Emissaries appointed by our great-uncle, who is the Sultan of this region."

"I see," the Mullah said. "Well, I must be moving on now, riding this stupid, stubborn foal here."

The other replied, "That's no foal! It's an adult male donkey!"

"Please don't say 'donkey'! Call him a foal rather."

"Please explain yourself."

"It's also a matter of breeding," Mullah asserted. "I have a very good reason for not calling him a donkey."

"What is that?" asked the emissary.

"Namely that fact that my father raised us together: sometimes we'd even sleep together in the stable. So we are as good as brothers, just like you."

DONKEY IS UNDER YOUR ASS

Nasruddin was riding contentedly on his little gray donkey, Karakacan, facing backward as usual. As he rode home, he started thinking about his donkey and became horny to fuck it.

When he arrived home and looked in the Karakacan's stall, though, the donkey was nowhere to be seen. "I wonder where that silly creature could have wandered off, this time," he thought, and left again immediately in search of his donkey.

Soon after the Mullah embarked upon his search for his missing donkey, he came across his neighbor Hussein who said, "Hey Mullah! Where are you going?"

"I've lost my donkey and am looking for it," said Nasruddin.

"But my dear fellow!" said Hussein. "Look! The donkey is right under your ass!"

Seeing that indeed his donkey was beneath him, Nasruddin shouted in joy and started the donkey moving in the same direction, rather than heading home.

"My friend, since you have found your donkey," Hussein said, "where are you off to now?"

"Yes, I've found the donkey all right," said Nasruddin, "but just around the corner, there is an excellent place for us to get reacquainted in private."

SON OF A DONKEY

Mullah Nasruddin was riding along on a male donkey, facing backward as per his usual style. A group of his students approached and, trying to evade them, he quickly dismounted the donkey and trotted on all fours beside it.

When the schoolchildren came up to him, Ismail pointed and said, "Why, hello, dear Mullah! What's going on here?"

"You are mistaken, child. I am not the Mullah."

"Really? Well, if you're not our teacher, Mullah Nasruddin, who exactly are you?"

"I'm just this donkey's foal."

"But Mullah," laughed Ismail, pointing at the donkey's dick, "this is a male donkey!"

Nasruddin replied, "My mama died, you see, and so now I am running with my father."

A LITTLE DAB'LL DO IT

Mullah Nasruddin once told his friend, Faik, "Every now and then my ass, Karakacan, is so stubborn that she refuses to move. What should I do?"

"I'll give you a salve," said Faik, "and any time your donkey does not want to move from the spot, smear a little of it on her butthole. That'll get her going."

Nasruddin agreed, so Faik gave him an ointment with ammonium salt.

One day, as Nasruddin was bringing firewood back with his donkey, the stubborn donkey stopped. She would go neither forward, backward, or sideways.

Quickly with his finger, Nasruddin applied some of the ointment on the beast's bottom. The sharp sting of the salt caused the poor donkey to bolt.

Karakacan ran away so fast that Nasruddin could not keep up, so he took the finger with some of the ointment still on it and stuck it up his own butt. The burning caused Nasruddin to also run so fast that he quickly caught up to the donkey as she galloped off to her stable.

When the donkey saw that the door of the stall was not open, she kept running. Nasruddin's wife started to follow the runaway ass, but then he screamed at her, "Woman! Forget the donkey! Grab hold onto me tight instead, or else I'll surely bore a hole through the whole countryside!"

THE BEAR IN THE PEAR TREE

Once the Mullah was chopping wood on the mountain when he saw an enormous bear bearing down on him. Quicker than he had ever done so in his childhood, he scrambled up a tall wild pear tree. The bear ambled over and lay down underneath, giving a drowsy grunt. Before long the bear was napping contentedly, his massive body slumped up against the trunk of the pear tree.

The Mullah waited for hours, but the beast did not stir. Dusk approached, and as the shadows became long, the Mullah hovered in the upper branches, shifting around to try to find a comfortable position. As the full moon rose, Nasruddin could see every detail of the bear's movement from above.

Eventually, the bear awoke and climbed up to eat some pears. As the bear ascended the tree, so did the Mullah move up from one higher branch to the next. The bear gobbled pears with his huge paws and great big teeth, quickly scaling until he was only one branch below the Mullah.

Finally, the Mullah was quivering in fear on the topmost branch with the bear just on the tree limb below him. To Nasruddin, it looked as if the bear was determined to eat every last pear in the tree. He knew that the bear was running out of fruit.

The bear had been hard at work, pulling and devouring the pears in the full light of the moon. At one point, the bear stretched out his paw until it almost touched the mouth of the Mullah.

Nasruddin, terrified that the bear was offering him a pear to share, shrieked in terror, "Oh! No, thank you, Mr. Bear! I don't really care to eat any of your pears! But thank you!"

The bear, startled at the sudden noise, lost its balance and fell with a terrifying roar, crashing branch by branch down to the ground, where it landed with an ominous thud. The creature lay there silent and motionless, never again to eat wild pears in the moonlight. Nasruddin just clung to the high branch, shivering.

In the morning, Nasruddin edged his way down the tree, thinking the bear must be dead. He hovered over the body until he was sure it was safe for him to jump down.

Now came the reward for a hard night's work. Retrieving his ax, the Mullah skinned the big bear and proudly draped its thick black fur over his shoulders.

As Nasruddin walked back into town, his new coat drew the admiration of all who happened to see his seemingly triumphant return from a great hunt.

HUMP-BACK CAMEL

One morning Nasruddin decided to leave town with a caravan. Musa, the caravan leader, offered to provide a camel for him.

The Mullah said, "Indeed, instead of going on foot, I prefer to ride your camel. That should make the trip much more pleasant." So, hoping for a comfortable journey, Mullah departed with the caravan.

A few hours later, suddenly the camel stumbled on a loose rock, threw Nasruddin to the ground, and stepped on his leg. Mullah wailed in pain, and Musa and other men came and helped him stand up again.

Hardly had he returned to his senses when he cried, "You Muslims! Look what harm this camel has brought me! Do me a favor, and hold it steady while I fuck the shit out of this wild beast!"

"But Mullah," Musa said, "Are you so unafraid of God that you would dare to fuck an animal?"

Nasruddin replied angrily, "What are you telling me? A camel can take revenge on a human being, but a human cannot retaliate?"

"It's not a matter of justice," answered Musa, "it's a matter of propriety."

"Your tribe doesn't seem to mind so much when a man fucks a boy for pleasure or a girl for passion," retorted the Mullah. "So why should you give half a shit if I want to mount a camel for punishment?"

COW OR DONKEY?

Fatima wanted milk for their children, so she nagged Nasruddin to get a cow so they might have a steady source on hand.

"My dear," countered Nasruddin, "I would gladly obtain for us a cow, but there is simply no room in the stable for one. It's just large enough for my little donkey, Karakacan, and considering that she is getting on in years, I want her to be as comfortable as possible."

The donkey's comfort, or lack thereof, hardly seemed a rationale to avoid getting a cow, so Fatima pressed her husband with her request until finally, he relented. He threw his leg over Karakacan's back and rode to market and, after considerable deliberation and bargaining, he chose a healthy-looking bovine and led her home.

Nasruddin was still sure that his donkey would suffer much, so he took the time on his way home with the cow to acquaint Allah with his predicament. He knelt on his prayer rug and, after bowing his head, he turned up his hands in appeal to the Almighty.

"Oh Allah," Mullah prayed, "Thou know that I love my little gray donkey and that she won't be at ease with a cow in the same stable. Dear Allah, if it is Thy will, please take the life of my cow, that my beloved little gray donkey, Karakacan, will be at peace." Having left the matter in God's hands, Nasruddin returned home, stabled and fed both animals, and went about the rest of his affairs.

The next morning, Mullah scurried out to the stable to see how his donkey managed overnight. To his shock, he found Karakacan had fallen and died. *"Ai vai,"* he wailed, heartbroken at the loss of his longtime friend.

Fatima, hearing his cries, ran to the window and called out, "Mullah, what is the matter?"

"It is nothing," Nasruddin muttered, then added under his breath bitterly, "nothing but my dear little donkey."

After Fatima closed the window, Nasruddin fell to his knees once again in supplication to God. "Oh, Allah, Thou art all-knowing and all-powerful. But can Thou not tell the basic difference between a cow and a donkey?"

HOLD THAT BEAR

Once Halil invited Nasruddin to hunt bears, and the Mullah reluctantly agreed. Halil quietly crawled in the small entrance to the bear cave, whispering, "Shhh, only the cubs are in the cave now."

Still outside, Mullah heard the nearby growl of a bear and ran away from the cave and behind a tree. Moments later, the mama bear appeared and meandered into the narrow cave opening.

Nasruddin quietly came up behind the bear. While it was midway through the cave entrance, the Mullah grabbed its tail and pulled back to keep it from entering further. The bear squirmed so that it became stuck in the opening. Unable to turn around or back up, the bear roared and kicked up clouds of dust in back and front.

Halil heard the noise behind him and yelled, "Nasruddin, why are you making such a racket out there, growling like a mama bear?"

"Shut up, stupid, and pray the tail holds," shouted the Mullah. "Otherwise, you'll find yourself in a real commotion *in* there!"

CAT SCRATCH FEVER

M ullah Nasruddin was serving as a judge when the village constable, Luqman, brought an ordinary-looking citizen before him in court and announced, "This pervert was caught screwing a cat."

The crowd in the court laughed nervously.

"Several eye-witnesses, including his wife and mother-in-law, can confirm the allegation," continued Luqman. "So, the defendant has no choice but to admit his vile act."

The Mullah was flabbergasted and beckoned the man forward. He asked, "First, you must explain to me me — that is, I have to ask you — how in the world did you manage to fuck a cat?"

The defendant replied, "First, I wrap the pussy in a felt cloak up to her belly. Then, I hold her mouth shut. Once the cat is subdued, I hold her from behind and procure admission."

Mullah said, "Really? That's all there is? That's how you do it?"

"Indeed, your Honor, I swear that is how I do it. In fact, it usually goes so well that I can repeat it twice in a row."

Mullah looked around, then he leaned in and beckoned for the man to come right up to the bench. He whispered, "Then what they say is true: never judge a book by its cover."

"What do you mean, Mullah?"

Mullah said, "You're my master in this game. I could never manage to accomplish it without getting my balls and thighs all scratched up. I've tried probably more than thirty times, in fact, but I never succeeded."

TEACH YOU A LESSON

O ne day, Mullah Nasruddin rode his little gray donkey, Karakacan, to a nearby village to visit a friend. Afterward, he decided to pray at the local *mescit*, an unadorned mosque typical in smaller towns and poor neighborhoods. So the Mullah tied up Karakacan behind the mescit and went inside.

A half hour later, after prayers were over, Nasruddin came out from the mescit and realized that he was horny. Seeing Karakacan tethered behind the temple, he mounted and started fucking her.

The imam leaving the mescit saw Nasruddin vigorously pumping his ass. He yelled, "Shame on you!" and spat disgustedly on the ground near the mosque.

Without breaking stride, the Mullah yelled back, "You should be grateful that I am busy with important business right now. If I didn't already have my hands full, I would teach you a hard lesson, not to spit near and defile a holy temple!"

THE DOG MINISTER

One day, when Mullah Nasruddin was walking toward the mosque, he saw a large dog at the door. Since religious Muslims consider dogs to be particularly unclean, he shooed away the dog, but instead, it ran right into the mosque and up to the pulpit, where it began to bark and howl.

"What an amazing thing," cried the Mullah. "This stupid creature must have been a former minister here!"

JUDGMENT DAY

Nasruddin adored his sweet-natured little lamb. Its gambols were a constant source of amusement to the Mullah and his family, and for several years he fed and cared for the happy creature with great affection.

The teahouse wags coveted Nasruddin's lamb and conspired to make him surrender it to their molars. The group considered one idea after another until finally, Ali came up with a scheme.

Ali approached Nasruddin once while he was tending his lone sheep out in the pasture. "Greetings, Nasruddin."

"Salaam, Ali. You have come to admire my fatted lamb," said Nasruddin.

"Indeed, Mullah," said Ali. "Your lamb is so delightful, so charming, so . . . succulent. I mean, so sweet! So it is indeed such a tragedy that it should be wasted, alas."

"What tragedy? Wasted? What are you talking about?"

"As has been prophesied, the world is coming to an end tomorrow. What a shame that such a gorgeous lamb should be wasted when Judgment Day comes."

"Shocking — I never heard about this! Are you sure that Judgment Day is tomorrow? May Allah save us!" cried Nasruddin.

Ali said, "Considering how well-informed you are, I'm surprised that you didn't know."

"My friend, thank you for letting me know about the end of days as foretold. I would never have known."

"Yes, Nasruddin," Ali assured him. "That is why it's too bad to waste your little sheep when you should cook and enjoy it. Everyone is planning to bring something special tonight to share at the picnic area by the lake. I'm sure your lamb would be ready in time for the final feast if you were to begin roasting it within the next couple of hours."

The Mullah was quite shocked at the sudden turn of events, but it seemed as if there were no way to save his beloved lamb, and so he resigned himself to the inevitable. With deep sadness in his voice, he said, "You're right, we may as well cook and eat it."

So Nasruddin slaughtered his beloved lamb and brought it to the picnic area at Lake Akşehir for the feast, and before long the poor creature was skinned and staked, and Nasruddin had the unhappy task of roasting it, turning the cooking meat on a spit over a small fire.

Meanwhile, Ali and the other men of the village came to the picnic and enjoyed themselves as they waited for Nasruddin's lamb to roast. Faruk suggested to them, "Let's go for a swim in the lake while the meal is cooking, and we shall return refreshed and have our feast of Nasruddin's little sheep."

The fellows tossed off their fezzes and turbans, sandals and clothes, into a pile and ran to the lake, hollering and diving into the fresh, pleasant water. For more than an hour they laughed and swam and splashed around while Nasruddin sat dejected, turning the roasting lamb on a spigot over and over again on the rotisserie as the sun sank lower toward the horizon.

After their pleasant interlude at dusk for Nasruddin's friends cavorting in the lake, they decided they had waited long enough. They were more than ready for their tasty meal of roast mutton.

As they came out of the water, dripping and naked, they laughed at Nasruddin's foolishness for believing that the end of the world was coming today. Ali said, "Now we shall confess everything to Nasruddin, and let him in on our wicked little trick on him, as we savor that delicious mutton."

But when they ran up to the spot on the bank where they had discarded their garments, they could find not a stitch of clothing there.

Covering themselves as best as they could, they ran to the fire pit, where they found Nasruddin happily smiling as he turned the roasting lamb over a now blazing fire, in which the men could make out charred and burnt remnants of their clothes, hats, and shoes.

"Nasruddin, you idiot, you imbecile, what have you done?" Ali yelled.

"Why, my friends, I didn't think you would mind in the least," Nasruddin answered innocently, "if I used your clothes for kindling to heat the fire to cook my beloved lamb. After all, if the end of the world is indeed today, and this is indeed our final feast, what need have any of you for clothing? Judgment Day is at hand, and you must go naked before your Creator."

PROTECTION FROM BEHIND

One day, Nasruddin was traveling past a farm when he saw a lame little donkey tied up to a post near a barn. He looked at the animal's rear, and it reminded him of other donkeys he had fucked, and he got horny, so he pounced on the hapless creature.

As the Mullah was fucking that hairy ass with gusto, the farmer who owned the donkey discovered them. He yelled, "Hey, what the fuck are you doing to my donkey?"

Nasruddin replied calmly, "Effendi, don't worry. This action will not harm your sweet little donkey. As a matter of fact, this protects him very effectively against attacks from behind by a vicious wolf."

NO IDEA HOW I GOT HERE

Mullah Nasruddin was coming home from the bazaar with his donkey, Karakacan, when he decided he wanted to plug her. He ducked down an alley and had just started to get into a rhythm when he noticed his nosy neighbor Faruk coming down the alleyway. The Mullah, wishing to appear discreet, threw his cloak over his head without missing a beat.

Faruk approached the donkey and her conspicuously cloaked rider. Curious, he lifted a corner of the cloak and said, "Hullo! Who's there?"

The Mullah replied, "Ah, my friend, Faruk, good thing you found me here! Look, please understand that I don't know who could have put me into this dire situation. In truth, I have no earthly idea at all how I got here."

A PROPER BIRD

In the market one day, Mullah Nasruddin came across a vendor selling exotic birds of various sorts, including a stork. Mullah had never seen this sort of bird before. He bought one of these peculiar long-legged, long-beaked birds at the market, and brought him home.

When he returned home, he set the bird down on a table and got out a cage he had which previously held two pigeons. Nasruddin looked at the new bird critically and realized that it would never fit in its cage. The proportions were all off.

"Poor queer thing," he sighed, "how did you ever grow into this wretched state?"

So he took a knife and trimmed the stork's beak and legs down to what looked like the right length. Then he put the stork in his cage and said, "Well, now not only do you finally fit, at least you look like a proper bird!"

ASK THE GOAT

Once, two criminals were on the run when they came to Akşehir and found themselves at the door of the Mullah's house. As the bandits argued about what to do next, they awakened Mullah Nasruddin and Fatima, who were sleeping sweetly upstairs. Through the open window, they could hear every word the two men said.

The first fellow suggested, "Why should we leave this town empty-handed? This house looks like the home of a mullah. We should slit the throat of that stupid goat in their yard."

"Okay, so why don't we do that, then sneak upstairs and stab the mullah in his sleep? Then we'll take whatever is in the house that's light in weight and heavy in price."

"Sounds like a plan to me. And if the mullah has a wife, we'll tie her up and gag her while we're going through their stuff."

"If she's not too homely, we ought to kidnap her."

"Sure, we could throw her in a sack onto the back of the donkey and take her like that."

"Good idea. We'll get her back to our place in the mountains and have our way with her."

"Great, we'll have plenty of fun tonight!"

At this, the Mullah jumped out of bed. He coughed and cleared his throat conspicuously while he scuffled about the bedroom, lighting several candles. Once the place was well lit, he then paced around the room, humming loudly.

The thieves, realizing that the mullah was awake and most likely able and ready to defend himself, looked blankly at each other, then took off for the hills.

Fatima needled him, "You chickenshit coward, you weren't brave enough to face those hoodlums to protect me. Shame on you."

The Mullah replied, "Why the fuck should you care? It would have been all fun and games for you, up there on the mountain playing around with those two nasty men. You had nothing to worry about here. The goat and I — we had some real skin in the game. If you don't believe me, just ask the goat."

BLAME THE ASS

In Akşehir, the deputy director of a particular state-owned factory was accused of obtaining free products on the pretext of using them on a "trial basis," all the while getting the government to reimburse him for the free products that he used. The workers and community leaders complained of corruption, and the village committee reprimanded him.

In his speech during a meeting of the entire factory staff, the deputy director made a practice of self-criticism. Logically convincing, he characterized his actions by saying, in short, "Mistakes were made."

At last, he concluded by saying, "How can you blame me? Actually, I wanted none of the various perquisites that were delivered to me from the people. Absolutely nothing. It was their initiative to send the things to me, and all I did was to sit in my office and receive them."

He had hardly finished speaking when he saw Nasruddin riding his donkey into the assembly hall, which immediately disrupted the order of the meeting, and drew everyone's attention to the Mullah. The deputy director yelled at him, "Nasruddin, this is outrageous. How dare you come riding in here on that donkey?"

"How can you blame me? I had nothing to do with the situation. Absolutely nothing," Nasruddin responded innocently, petting his donkey.

"Actually, I wanted to go somewhere else entirely. It's all this stupid ass's fault. It was the donkey who wanted to bring me in here; all I did was just to sit on her and let her have her way."

THE DONKEY IS FINE

Nasruddin was traveling, plodding along on his old gray donkey when he crossed paths with an arrogant young man riding a fancy, charming, well-groomed horse.

The fellow haughtily waved and called out, "How does it feel to ride a donkey, old Mullah?"

"Quite fine, thank you," replied Nasruddin. "It feels just as good as you must feel — an ass, riding a horse."

LET'S HOPE IT'S NOT TRUE

One day, Nasruddin rode his little gray donkey into the woods to chop timber. He tethered Karakacan to a large rock and wandered off to scout for suitable trees to fell. While he was away and not paying attention, wolves attacked and ate his donkey.

Sadly Nasruddin returned to his village. At the edge of town, he saw two of his students, Ismail and Mahmoud, and asked, "Have you heard any rumors lately?"

Ismail answered, "Not really, Mullah. What sort of rumor?"

"Well, has anyone in town been talking about the wolves that have just eaten Mullah Nasruddin's donkey?"

"Sorry, Mullah," said Mahmoud, "but we've been playing here for hours, and nobody's said a word about wolves or your donkey."

"Well, that's a relief," sighed the Mullah, "Let's hope that the rumor you haven't heard might not be true."

FEEDING THE DONKEY YOGURT

Nasruddin's hairy ass lost a great deal of weight, and so one day he asked Hussein, "What am I to do? How can I possibly feed this poor scrawny donkey of mine to keep her alive?"

Hussein advised him, "Just put some yogurt on your cock and then plug it into the donkey's pussy. That will sustain her."

Nasruddin thought that was an excellent idea for a remedy. When he got home, he took a jar of curds to the stall and coated his erection with it. After numerous doses of yogurt were introduced in this manner, when he plugged his cock into the donkey, he got too excited and came. Then he pulled out of the donkey and yelled at his cock, "You hotheaded boy! Did you really just fuck this pitifully emaciated creature? You've never had sex with such a skinny donkey!"

Ungrateful son of a donkey

One day, the Mullah's donkey, Karakacan, gave birth to a foal. Believing himself the father, Mullah thought, *Since I now have two donkeys, I shall send my son to a teacher to instruct him, so that he will be taught, he will learn to read, and he will come to teach me.*

When it was old enough to walk, Nasruddin took the young donkey to the schoolteacher, Halil, and told him, "This, my son, wants an education. Please tutor him so that he will be less of a fool than me."

Halil replied in astonishment, "What are you asking me? That I should teach this son of a donkey of yours?"

Nasruddin nodded.

"Well, pay me up front my proper tuition fee, plus room and board. Then I'll gladly accept your son as a pupil and teach him everything I know."

So Nasruddin counted out to Halil an exorbitant payment. The teacher took the reins of the donkey and told the Mullah, "Now go in peace. Do not worry. I will take care of your child and teach him well. I will treat him as if he were my child."

After Mullah left, Halil said to his wife, "That Nasruddin has gone completely bonkers. I have never seen such idiocy. Everyone knows that you can't teach the son of an ass not to be an ass."

The next day, Halil took Nasruddin's son of a donkey to the cattle market and sold it.

Nasruddin patiently waited a week, and then impatiently another three days, then he went to the teacher. When he arrived, he saw that his son was not anywhere to be found, so he asked Halil, "Where has your student gone?"

The teacher replied, "He is not here. I sent him not far from here, him and his friend, on an errand. But rest assured, he is progressing well in his studies and is very popular with the other students."

"That's good to hear. I was afraid he would misbehave with you as often as his mother has troubled me," said the Mullah. "I'm going now, but I'll return to check on him in ten days. "

Halil said, "Go home and enjoy yourself. Your son has told us he lacks for nothing. Rest assured he is in excellent hands."

So Nasruddin walked home, and in ten days he returned to Halil's house. When he arrived, he saw that his son was not there, so he asked, "Where has my son, your student, gone?"

Halil embraced the Mullah and said proudly, "Congratulations! Your son turned out to be one of my finest students. Simply brilliant. He graduated with honors."

Mullah was delighted to learn that his son was a diligent student, and he asked the teacher, "When will I be able to see him? I have missed him all these weeks."

Halil replied, "In fact, your son is no longer here. I sent him to another city to instruct other students of mine. Your son has become a very accomplished legal scholar, and you should be very proud of him."

"I am indeed a proud father, Halil, just as you must be a proud teacher of such an outstanding pupil. But I would like to be able to see him and talk with him about certain domestic affairs. The boy has not seen his father in months now, and I am certain he would like to see his mother as well."

"Nasruddin, now that your son has become an authority on certain aspects of law, his time is truly at a premium. Go back home now, and I will write him a letter to ask that you may come to him. Then I'll write you a letter, and let you know when and where you can meet him."

Nasruddin said, "Okay then, I'll just wait to hear from you."

The Mullah returned home. He waited many days and weeks, but he saw no letter from the teacher and no greeting from his son. He went to the teacher and said to him, "Well, Halil, here I am."

The teacher said, "Just today, I was going to write you a letter to give you a very nice message from your son."

Mullah said, "Really? Come on. Tell me what he wrote to you."

Halil informed him, "It's absolutely fabulous news. You won't believe it."

"Try me."

"Your son wrote that last week he and his entourage moved to the capital city. He has just been named as the Sultan."

This news well pleased Nasruddin, who said, "I shall now go and visit my son."

Halil replied, "All right, go see your son. He is in a city called Woden. But when you arrive there, do not tell anyone that you are his father, for he now holds significant title and prestige. When you see him in court, definitely don't identify yourself as his parent. It would be considered the height of rudeness. Also, if you speak to him at the wrong moment, he'll be sure to have you whipped within an inch of your life."

Nasruddin became very angry and declared, "I'll go see him and talk to him about anything I like, and I am not afraid of him attacking me!"

So Nasruddin traveled to see the Sultan in the great city of Woden, where there was a famous king. Mullah entered the palace and came to the royal assembly. He saw the king, bowed, and sat down among the people.

Then he looked at the king, and whispered aloud, "Ahh, this is my son!"

Then he turned to other courtiers nearby, and said again, "Ahh, this is my son!" A few persons heard and reacted with shock.

The Mullah then spoke aloud, "Yes, indeed, no doubt that is my son."

Most of the courtiers heard it, but no one thought much of it, or perhaps they thought that the strange mullah was confused. But he continued repeating the same words, "This is my son."

Shortly one of the courtiers came up to Nasruddin and asked him, "Pardon me, kind Mullah, what did you say?"

Nasruddin stood, pointed to the Sultan, and said, "This indeed is my son."

This comment scandalized everyone in court, and the enraged Sultan declared, "Lock this madman up!"

Now Mullah was seized and bound with ropes on his arms and legs. As they were trying to subdue him, he said, "The children of donkeys have no gratitude. You, Sultan, are you not the son of my ass? Have I not made you and given you to the teacher so that he could teach you? Now you get a royal title, and I'm tied up. If you let me go, I swear I'll go right to your mother and cut off her tail!"

The Sultan became even angrier and ordered his men, "Take him out of here and execute him immediately!"

The vizier, a sagacious man, intervened. He whispered to the Sultan, "I believe, my Lord, that it is better if you let this fool go because clearly, he does not know what he's saying. No man with any brains can utter such words in your Majesty's presence." Thus Mullah was freed from his shackles, taken to the city limits, and released.

Finally, he returned dejectedly to Halil and told him, "Your words are true. The children of donkeys are inconsiderate ingrates. The son of my ass got the kingship, and while in court, he had his soldiers grab and restrain me. Now I am going to his mother and cut off her cursed tail. If you want it, I'll give it to you for free."

Halil said, "Fine. You should cut her tail off because she taught her son no manners whatsoever. Then if you want to give me the tail, I'll use it until I die."

So Nasruddin went out to the stable, cut off Karakacan's tail, and delivered it to the teacher.

You go first

One day the Mullah was at the side of a brook, relieving his bladder. While he was washing up and performing his ablutions, a donkey came up and peed right next to him, opening her vagina.

Just at that moment, Nasruddin's friend, Faik, happened to be passing by when he saw Nasruddin and greeted him, "Why, hello there, gentle Mullah!"

The Mullah realized that it looked like he was in a compromising situation, standing up with his pants down around his ankles, with the donkey standing next to him with her pussy exposed.

So he said, "Faik, I swear, I hadn't done it yet! But please, my friend, help yourself! I insist — you go first. Step right up and plug her!"

Slow and steady

Karakacan, Nasruddin's old gray donkey, was moving ever so slowly down the road. She had gotten very feeble and could only move one leg at a time, meaning, she was moving slower than a man could walk backward. This pace gave the Mullah plenty of time to contemplate where he had just been.

One day, while on donkey-back, he came across his friend Halil. "Wherever are you going so leisurely, effendi?"

"I'm on my way to lead Friday prayers," replied Nasruddin.

Halil remarked, "But Mullah — today is only Tuesday!"

"I know exactly what day it is, thank you very much," Nasruddin replied, pointing to his devoted but decrepit donkey, "but with a tired old ass like mine, I must leave on Tuesday to arrive in time for the Friday service!"

GRACEFUL EXIT

One day, Nasruddin was walking in the woods when he came upon a beautiful gray-dappled jenny-mule quietly munching on some hay. He approached her from behind, and because she reminded him of the jenny he used to screw as a boy, he became excited and mounted her.

Before long, just as he was about to finish, a burly fellow came along and asked him, "What the fuck do you think you're doing to my mule?"

"Brother, can't you see my predicament?" replied the Mullah breathlessly. "It is obvious that I'm stuck here. I'm just waiting until she releases me from her trap. I've been trying for some time now to get out of this cursed animal — but as you must know, she is a tricky, stubborn one. Kindly give me one minute more, and I think I'll be able to extricate myself from her clutches."

TAIL IS CLOSE AT HAND

When Nasruddin took his donkey, Karakacan, to sell at the market one morning, he noticed its tail was dirty and matted, so he cut it off and put it in his saddlebag.

At the market, he gave the donkey to the broker, but nobody was interested in the beast. Finally, a prospective customer came up to examine it and asked, "What kind of donkey is this, that doesn't have a tail?"

"If you're truly interested, then let's make a deal right now," said the Mullah, as he patted his bag with the donkey tail inside. "Trust me: the tail has not gone far away. And whoever buys the donkey can have it at absolutely no extra charge."

ALTRUISTIC IMPULSE

Once, Mullah Nasrudin saw a poor little donkey that was stuck knee-deep in a mud pit. Unable to resist his urges, he immediately pounced on the vulnerable animal and began fucking it.

Just then, Hussein came by and saw Nasruddin steadily humping the donkey. He called out, "Mullah, what in the world are you doing?"

Without missing a stroke, Nasruddin replied, "Hussein, I found this lame donkey helplessly caught in the mud. Having no other sturdy tools on hand, the only way to rescue her from certain peril is to lift her out of the bog with my big hard cock. But don't worry, my friend: to assure you of my selflessness, I declare that you can have the reward for saving her life."

FOUR FARTS OF THE DONKEY

Nasruddin rode his little grey donkey Karakacan one day to chop firewood in the forest near Akşehir. After tethering her to a small sapling, he climbed up a nearby mulberry tree. It wasn't easy for the middle-aged man to do such work, but he made his way up slowly and carefully. By the time he reached the high branch, he was panting and sweating, but he cautiously edged out onto the thick limb he wanted to cut down. When finally he caught his breath, he pulled the ax from his belt, turned toward the tree trunk, and began chopping at the base of the branch on which he sat.

Several minutes later, the village schoolteacher, Halil, walked by. When he heard the chopping, he looked up and noticed what the Mullah was doing. Halil called out, "Nasruddin, you are cutting the wrong side of the branch. Be careful — you will unquestionably fall if you keep chopping it that way!"

Nasruddin scoffed at the man, "Perhaps you know schoolchildren's books, my dear Halil, but not trees. I have been cutting wood since long before you were teaching school. Do you take me for a fool that I should believe you, or are you a mystical seer who can predict the future?"

"Nasruddin effendi, you are absolutely going to fall if you cut the limb that way! Just look where you are sitting and where you are axing."

"And you, Halil, should look where you are walking," replied Nasruddin. "Those who stroll along with their eyes in the treetops are likely to stub their toes on the roots."

Halil shrugged and left Nasruddin to resume his chopping. A few moments later, the limb cracked, gave way, and crashed with Nasruddin to the ground.

"Vai! Vai!" groaned Nasruddin. "Big head, big headache," he said, rubbing the lump swelling under his turban.

Brushing aside the hurt from his bruises and scratches, Nasruddin was so astonished at the schoolteacher's prediction coming true that he limped quickly to catch up with the sage who had accurately foretold his imminent disaster.

"Tell me, oh great seer Halil!" he called. "How could you have known beforehand of my fall from the tree? Your prophecy has been fulfilled! You are a prophet and the son of a prophet!" Nasruddin caught up to the schoolteacher and grabbed his cloak. When Halil turned to face him, the Mullah dropped to his knees, clasped his hands, and said, "You must reveal to me now, all-knowing Halil! I implore you to speak the truth of my future: when will I die?"

However much he tried, Halil could not convince Nasruddin that he was no prophet and would not foretell his death. After several minutes of haranguing by Nasruddin, however, Halil became so irritated that he blurted out, "I predict that you shall die when . . . when your pathetic donkey is carrying you and farts four times!" And with that, the teacher turned on his heels and strode off.

Bruised and shaken and unable to work any longer, Nasruddin dusted himself off, adjusted his turban, grabbed his ax, and swung his leg over his little gray donkey's back to head home.

After a while, Karakacan finished the last bit of oats in her feed bag, and farted. Nasruddin remembered Halil's prediction with a growing sense of horror. "Aman, aman! If what was foretold is true, I am one-fourth dead," he said, thinking this farting thing had gone far enough.

Farther down the road, Karakacan began to think about more food she would have at home, and farted again. The noise shocked Nasruddin. "Vai, vai!" shuddered the Mullah. "I am now half-dead!"

Soon after, Karakacan began thinking of the fresh water she would drink when they returned home. She was thirsty from the day's work, and farted again. "May Allah save me!" wailed Nasruddin, "Now I have become three-quarters expired!"

The doomed Mullah tried to distract her from anything that might make her fart again. He spoke soothing sibilant words and sang odes to his beloved donkey. He tried to think how he could possibly plug or muzzle the donkey's ass for the rest of her (and his) days to keep her from farting again one final, fatal time.

Ahead on the road, just outside the village, the Mullah could make out the gruff voices of men shouting orders to their donkeys and the clop-clop of small hooves. Karakacan's little gray ears pricked up and turned forward, and she sniffed the air. The sound piercing Nasruddin's heart, the fourth fart of the donkey seemed as if she were laughing, long and loud.

He dropped his ax, clutched his chest, and declared loudly, "That's it! That's all! I have run out of farts. I am completely dead! I am perished! I am deceased! I am no more! I am so dead. Really, really dead and gone. Allah be praised."

He dropped to the earth once again — this time, taking care to lay himself out comfortably flat on the ground.

Nasruddin's friends, Mali, Jafar, and Faik, who were the men traveling with their donkeys, heard Nasruddin's cries and rushed to the scene. They tried to revive him, but Nasruddin was unresponsive and limp as an empty saddlebag. "He was shouting that he was dead," observed Faik, "and if anyone should know if he were dead or not, it's Nasruddin."

They sadly loaded the dead Nasruddin on his donkey's back and solemnly carried him to his house. There his body was washed, wrapped in a simple shroud, placed in a casket, and lifted toward the graveyard.

As the group made their way slowly out of the village, many more mourners joined along the way. Halfway along the funeral route, the road forked in three different directions, and the procession came to a halt, unsure of the best path to the cemetery.

Mali first spoke up. "I can tell you for certain that the shortest and best route is to the left."

Jafar said, "Without doubt, the right fork is the smoother way to the graveyard."

Faik countered, "The road straight ahead is less dusty."

In minutes an argument broke out among the mourners as to the better route to bury their unfortunate friend.

Just as it seemed that the funeral-goers were about to come to blows, Nasruddin sat up in the coffin and cleared his throat. "Listen, friends, when I was alive, I always used to take the road to the left to get to the cemetery."

The villagers, long accustomed to letting the Mullah have the final word, took the left fork and made their way to the gravesite.

The funeral procession removed Nasruddin's remains from the casket from the bier and lowered it into a freshly dug grave. The service, conducted with proper respect for the Mullah's exalted position in the community, included many lengthy and stirring eulogies and much weeping and beating of chests, in the poignant memory of their beloved Nasruddin. The interment at last concluded and the mourners left the Mullah to mull over his untimely and tragic death, resting in the eerie quietude of the cemetery.

Just as the silence started to press in upon Nasruddin uncomfortably, far off in the distance, he could hear a heavenly tinkling sound. Nasruddin thought, *Surely that must be the sound of the angel of death, Azrael, as he approaches me in my Final Judgment! If Azrael looks in this grave and sees me laid out like a corpse, doubtless he will deem me doomed and spirit me away!*

The sound was actually an approaching group of potters transporting their wares to market, leading their camels laden with colorful pots, bowls, vases, dishes, and other artful handcrafted pottery of every sort. As the caravan drew near, the bells around the camels' legs chimed louder in the Mullah's ears. Dumbstruck with fear, Nasruddin shivered in his newly dug grave.

Nasruddin could not hear, over the tinkling of camel bells and the dreadful chattering of his teeth, the low patter of the potters' voices and the rhythmic clacking of ceramics as the group made their way through the cemetery on camelback. He thought, *I must stand up and shout to the Angel when he arrives, to make sure he knows I am not actually dead!* His knees knocked so hard that he could barely get to his feet. It took every bit of courage he could muster to bring himself to stand up and peer out from his newly dug grave.

From ground level, Nasruddin looked around and realized it was not the angel of death who was approaching; it was a band of dirty ceramics salesmen — telling crude jokes — and the potters' filthy camels. In a flash, his fear became outrage.

Nasruddin fumed, thinking, *Imagine the indecency of using the graveyard as a shortcut for camels, in the sacred burial ground of myself and my family — and on my funeral day!* This was an insult and a shame!

Nasruddin's anger flared, and just as the caravan reached within a few feet, he scrambled up out of his grave, ready to confront the men. Still dressed in his burial clothes, Nasruddin roared like a wounded elephant, as he waved his arms and swore unrepeatable insults at the scoundrels who had defiled his funeral.

His sudden outburst, unfortunately, startled the head potter of the caravan, a big bear of a man who was nonetheless very superstitious. When the man saw the shrouded apparition jump up from the grave, screeching and waving his arms like a wraithlike djinn, he jumped back into the other men, knocking them over and spooking the camels, which in their confusion and terror reared and fled for their lives, scattering and shattering pottery every which way.

The potters, unable to control the runaway camels, saw their wares in shards all around the graveyard. Turning to the Mullah, the potters unleashed their fury on him, the unwitting cause of the loss of their caravan's lode. Sparing none of God's vengeance on him and offering none of His mercy, they thrashed him until he was black and blue from turban to toes, then dumped his body unceremoniously in his own grave, leaving him for dead.

Sore, swollen, and stiff, Nasruddin lay in his shallow grave for what seemed like an eternity. Finally, when he was sure the potters had left, he decided to try to arise from his near-death experience.

As he shakily got to his feet, he spotted a huge, scruffy, dirty mongrel sniffing around the headstone of his new grave, recently decorated with a lovely wreath and other flowers. Religious Muslims consider dogs to be particularly unclean. Adding insult to injury, to Nasruddin's dismay, he watched the dog lift his leg and water the flowers. *White dogs, black dogs,* Nasruddin reflected, *all are born of bitches.*

Waving his arms, he yelled at the dog, "Scram, you horrid mutt! Have some respect for the deceased, I say. Stop that at once!" The nasty dog faced Nasruddin, bared its sharp teeth, growled and snarled and snapped, poised to attack.

Nasruddin jumped backward in fear, then kept backing up. In a soothing voice, he said, "Down, boy! Nice doggy, nice doggy! Terribly sorry to bother you. You just do your business as you please. I'll just stay right back here and mind my own." The dog finished and scampered off to defile other gravesites.

By now Nasruddin had experienced quite enough of death and wanted no more of it. Sore in every pore of his body and humiliated beyond comprehension, he wrapped himself in the dirty, bloody shroud, crawled out of his grave, and hobbled home.

Fatima, shocked by her husband's frightful appearance but of course happy to see him alive, hugged him warmly and tended to his bruises and cuts. As he sat soaking in a hot bath, she said, "So, I hesitate to ask, but tell me: where were you?"

Nasruddin replied wearily, "I died, and was laid to rest."

Fatima clucked her tongue, "Ai vai! So tell me: how was the afterlife?"

"Well," the Mullah replied, "things are not so bad, except that you must take great care not to frighten the potters' camels."

PART VI

Adventures around the Village

HERE COMES THE JUDGE

Nasruddin and his student Imad were walking back to town one evening when they witnessed Bekri, the local judge, romping around nearly naked in his vineyard. The elderly magistrate was singing bawdy songs merrily and carrying a jug of wine, from which he would take a swig every so often and then begin singing again.

Shortly Bekri gasped loudly and dropped to the ground as if struck dead. When Nasruddin and Imad went to check that the man was all right, they found him face down in a drunken stupor. Nearby they found the judge's costly silk cloak and turban, apparently abandoned sometime earlier, which Nasruddin took. For fun, they pulled Bekri's underpants down to his ankles, then returned home.

When Bekri awoke the next day, he made his way home in disgrace. He called his servant and told him, "Be on the lookout for the clothes. Go find the fellow who stole them and bring him before me at court."

Sure enough, soon Nasruddin could be found strutting around town in his new finery. The servant collared Nasruddin and brought him to Luqman the *bekche*, who promptly escorted him before Bekri while court was in session. Luqman read the charge: "Nasruddin, you are accused of stealing a cloak and turban."

The Mullah immediately stated his case to the judge, speaking loudly so that everyone in the room could hear. "Your Honor, last night I was walking with Imad, my disciple, past your vineyard when we came across some debased, drunken fellow, running around stark naked, chugging wine from a jug and singing vulgar lyrics, the likes of which I'm sure your Honor has never heard before in his life."

A murmur rose from among the people sitting in the scandalized courtroom.

"You don't say," said Bekri at last.

"I do say," continued Nasruddin. "The unfortunate sot was so intoxicated that before long he heaved and pitched and collapsed in a pool of his waste at the bottom of a sewage ditch with his trousers around his ankles. Such a sinful, disgusting man!"

"Please spare me your moralizing, Nasruddin. Go on."

"In any matter, even though I could not make out the drunken man's identity, as he had fallen flat face-down in the gutter, I could see that he had discarded his cloak and turban by the side of the road. Knowing that many thieves and ruffians inhabit the roads, I thought it best that we take the fine garments to keep them safe and clean."

"Of course, Nasruddin. That was indeed quite thoughtful."

"And to teach that wicked rascal a lesson, Imad fucked him."

Bekri's eyes widened, and his nostrils flared. "Oh, really? That might have been taking it a bit too far, don't you think?"

"The situation demanded we mete out appropriate punishment. I believe, however, that we must consider the likelihood that this grave sinner who trespassed on your treasured vineyard must have been an infidel reprobate from some other place, because as you know drinking alcohol is forbidden to all true believers, and only true believers live in your jurisdiction. Would you agree, your Honor?"

"I cannot disagree with your assessment that the man was not from here, Nasruddin. Considering that you have already worn the clothes, keep them. I wish to hear nothing more of this matter — case dismissed!"

HE GETS THE JOKE

Nasruddin went to the bazaar and bought a large, ornate ceramic urn. In order to get home, he had to traverse the Akşehir River. When he arrived at the river, he noticed that other people were standing at the riverbank, afraid to risk entering the water. Since the rains were heavy that year, the current was powerful.

So the Mullah knelt and prayed, "God, if Thou art willing to help me bring this lovely, costly urn safely across the river, I will offer Thou a pot filled with a delicious rice dish."

Having made his solemn vow, the Mullah carefully hoisted the urn atop his head and made his way through the rushing stream. When finally he reached the other side, he exclaimed in glee, "Haha, look how clever that I am! I have cheated even God!"

He had not even walked five more steps before he tripped on a tree root. The pot flew from his hands, fell to the ground, and broke into a hundred pieces. Nasruddin raised his arms, looked up, and called out, "Oh dear God, do Thou not understand a simple joke?"

CULTURAL ETIQUETTE

Tamerlane invited Mullah Nasruddin to a banquet to receive the Emperor's blessing. Nasruddin took his student Imad and went to the palace. He greeted Tamerlane, who bade him and Imad to sit down.

Nasruddin saw how Tamerlane, who walked with a limp from a lame leg, rested his foot under a pillow while sitting, and the Mullah did so as well.

As Tamerlane noticed that the Mullah was mimicking him, he said, "When I do that, I have a reason for doing so. And besides, I am the Emperor, after all!" He asked the Mullah, "How is your behavior here different from that of a donkey?"

Nasruddin only replied, "By this cushion on which we sit!"

After they had eaten the first course, Tamerlane belched loudly. The Mullah acted affronted, "My Lordship! Is it not a shame to do such a thing?"

Tamerlane replied, "In the land where I am from, this is not considered a disgrace."

So the Mullah let out a loud fart, and Tamerlane complained, "Are you not ashamed?"

Mullah retorted, "In the part of our country where I come from, we do not see this as disgraceful!"

At the conclusion of the meal, sorbet was served, then everyone rose from their seats and left.

On their way home, Imad asked the Mullah, "What does it mean when the Emperor farts?"

Nasruddin replied calmly, "That's obvious," replied the Mullah. "When the Emperor farts, it means that the community needs to take a shit!"

SWIMMING INSTRUCTION

One day Mullah Nasrudin was walking along a riverbank when he decided to do a necessity.

Once he'd cleaned himself, he stood up and watched his buoyant pile float away by itself, meandering down the stream.

Nasruddin gasped with disbelief, and exclaimed, "Ai vai! Undoubtedly the end of the world is nigh! Surely Judgment Day has come upon us! For this unclean thing teaches us how to swim and stay afloat in the water!"

HENS IN THE HAMMAM

A group of older boys liked to play tricks on their teacher, Mullah Nasruddin, or at least they tried to play jokes on him. Like all kids, and like plenty of adults, the Mullah loved a good prank, and the boys knew that Nasruddin was likely to discern their hidden intents and cleverly turn the trick upside down on them, and so everyone had a good time.

Nasruddin made a point of visiting the hammam every Thursday morning. It was a sociable habit of his to spend this special time at the Turkish baths steaming, sudsing, soaping, and relaxing, as Mesut, the hammamji brought bowl after bowl of steaming hot water for his tub.

So the young men hatched what they hoped would be a foolproof scheme to trick Nasruddin into paying the hammam fee for all of them. Each boy brought an egg secretly into the hammam and hid it between his legs under the towel as they sat down in the steam room.

After Nasruddin paid his fee and changed into his towel, he walked to the central basin. He was surprised that instead of the noisy boys he expected, they were all sitting together on one sadir, conspicuously quiet and cross-legged.

Nasruddin settled into his usual seat and relaxed. He knew his voice sounded full and rich in the hammam, and he hummed a little, testing the sound. He was glad the children were acting well-behaved so that he could hear his marvelous voice better, and he drifted into a humming reverie.

Nasruddin's meditation in the baths was interrupted by one of the boys, Mehmet, who said, "I have an idea, Mullah! Let's imagine that we are all fowls, and can lay eggs. The chicken who fails to produce an egg will have to pay the bath fee for us all!" The rest of the boys quickly chimed in their agreement and cajoled Nasruddin to join the dare. After some persuasive bragging and nagging, Nasruddin eventually agreed to the wager.

After a moment, Mehmet cackled nervously, flapped his arms a few times, sat up, reached under his towel, and held out an egg. Then Ismail giggled nervously and pulled an egg from between his legs. After six eggs were laid in this manner for all six boys, they taunted Nasruddin, "Your turn now, Mullah! You must show us your contribution to the poultry flock." The boys were making every effort to refrain from laughter, but when Mehmet blurted, "The Mullah lays — or the Mullah pays!" the whole group of boys erupted into hilarity.

The Mullah laughed with the boys for a minute, and then suddenly he threw his head back, and crowed loudly, his voice reverberating through the hammam.

The dumbstruck boys were taken aback as they watched Nasruddin flap his arms, clucking and crowing.

Nasruddin flailed and bobbed and pumped his arms and legs, and as he stood up, his bath towel dropped to the floor. The boys squealed and pretended to look away, as Nasruddin scuttled around, still doing a very convincing rooster imitation, then seemed to notice suddenly that his towel had fallen.

"Here are two large, hairy eggs — twice as many and twice the size what any of you boys produced from between your legs." He retrieved his towel and redraped himself modestly as he sat back down, sporting a huge smile. "And besides, among all these small hens, shouldn't there be at least one large, mature cock as well?"

The boys clucked and good-naturedly paid their bath fees themselves, and everyone had a hearty laugh.

A SOLEMN VERSE

One day in the mosque, Mullah Nasruddin pulled the mosque prayer leader's ear, just as he bowed in prayer. Ignoring the insult, the prayer leader recited the most solemn prayer of the Quran, namely the so-called "Throne Verse."

The Mullah declared, "If pulling your ear makes you recite something as grave as the Throne Verse, I can hardly imagine what you would decide to chant if someone grabs you by your balls."

DIETARY RESTRICTIONS

One day during Lent, Nasruddin was traveling alone and hungry, when he saw a Christian man sitting by the side of the road by himself, eating some delicious-smelling roasted meat on a platter. Without hesitation, he sat down and prepared to eat with him.

The Christian said, "Mullah! Surely, you must know that Muslims are prohibited from eating the meat of the animals we have killed."

Mullah replied, "Just you never mind all those arcane dietary restrictions for folks of religions other than your own." He looked around to make sure they were still alone. "Let's simply say that I am now among the Muslims, just as you are now among the Christians!"

WHY HOLES ARE BELOW

One day as Nasruddin was preaching in the mosque, he declared, "Oh true believers! Oh Muslims! We must commend and give thanks to Allah for His infinite wisdom. For example, For example, God has blessed us by not attaching our assholes to our foreheads instead of our bottoms."

The congregation was baffled. Hussein spoke up, "Mullah, whatever do you mean by that?"

Nasruddin explained, "If that were the case, all day long we would be wiping feces from our faces!"

AT LEAST ONE OF THEM

Early one morning, Nasruddin went out hunting and shot two quails. He brought them to his wife and told her to prepare the fowls because he wanted to invite his wealthy friend Aslan to supper to impress him.

Fatima took the birds, and she plucked and prepared them. As she was roasting the quails, the smell was irresistibly delicious. Since Fatima had very little self-control, she could not stop herself from tasting the quail to make sure it was just as delectable as it smelled — just a small piece, so that Nasruddin would never notice.

She sampled the quail, and tasted it once more, and nibbled it again. Finally, she had eaten both quails. When Fatima realized what she had done, she became very upset and did not know at first what she should do.

At dusk, when the two men arrived, Fatima seated Aslan at the table. Then she took the Mullah to the kitchen, gave him a long knife, and asked him to take it outside to grind it so that it could adequately slice the bread.

Once Nasruddin was grinding the knife on the stone in back, she whispered to Aslan, "Sir, you are in grave danger by staying here! The Mullah has a terrible habit. Every time he invites someone to eat a meal with us, he becomes insanely jealous and cuts off the balls of the guest."

Aslan's face turned pale as porcelain. "You don't say."

"I do say. Can't you hear how keenly he sharpens his knife out back? It's so sad! The last three men who tried to have dinner with us will have no more children."

"God save me!" Aslan yelped with fear and quickly ran out the door.

Fatima waited a few moments to give Aslan a head start. Then she calmly walked to the kitchen, grabbed the platter, and ran to her husband still grinding the blade of his knife. She showed him the empty dish and shrieked, "Hoca, your friend has stolen both of the quails and gone!"

Immediately the Mullah ran out into the street after his friend, brandishing the knife in his hand, crying out, 'Please, please, my friend, be fair: just let me have one of them! Just one will be enough! Please, one will do . . ."

Aslan looked back, saw the huge knife in Nasreddin's hand, and then he ran away even faster, shouting back, "If you can catch me, then you will undoubtedly have both!"

Nickname warning

One day, as Nasruddin was preaching a sermon at the mosque, he declared, "Oh true believers, heed my advice well: If you have a son born to you, do not ever name him 'Eyup.'"

Someone in the congregation asked, "What is your reason for that, Mullah?"

"Over time, people will shorten 'Eyup' to a nickname and, inevitably, your boy will come to be called 'Ip.'"

Hidden meanings

The famed dervish Sari Saltuk Baba came to visit Mullah Nasruddin at his home. As the Mullah showed him around the house, Baba asked, "Tell me, Nasruddin. Do you own this property?"

"As for me," replied the Mullah cryptically, "I own only three things: my dick and two balls."

Saltuk Baba was astonished at the audacious response. *Surely the wise Mullah couldn't have meant literally what he said,* he thought, so Baba interpreted the statement symbolically. By the two testicles, he reasoned, Nasruddin might have meant "divine knowledge" and "rightful action." But Saltuk drew a blank trying to interpret the hidden meaning of the penis.

The Mullah, realizing the question in the dervish's mind, said, "The one issue you are trying to understand is: purity of heart."

Flea-free home

Once there were so many spiders, fleas, and bedbugs in Nasruddin's house that he could stand it no longer and left home for the day.

When the Mullah later arrived back home, he saw that his house was on fire. The conflagration was so intense that he could only stand and watch his home destroyed by the flames.

Oddly, he acted delighted, clapping his hands, jumping up and down, giggling like a schoolboy.

Hussein, his neighbor, asked, "Nasruddin, your house is burning down, and you are standing around as if it's the happiest day of your life. What the fuck is the matter with you?"

Mullah guffawed and said, "Hussein, my dear friend, this is the most auspicious of auspicious days. The house is burning down! Now once and for all, I'm finally rid of all those fucking pests and bugs." And he continued to laugh until the last timber fell.

His awful mistake

Aslan, the Mullah's neighbor, died unexpectedly. The relatives beseeched Nasruddin to perform the proscribed rites, and he agreed willingly. He accompanied them as the body was washed, wrapped in a shroud, and placed in a casket. He led the procession to the cemetery, accompanied by the appropriate prayers, and gave a touching eulogy. At the conclusion of Aslan's somber memorial service, the group left the coffin on a bier.

As the mourners were preparing to leave, Nasruddin requested of them, "Friends, is it not fair that you pay me for my participation in the funeral?"

The group discussed the matter and agreed that for the Mullah to ask for payment after the service, not before, was inappropriate, and so Aslan's family gave him half his requested fee before dispersing.

Once everyone had departed from the gravesite, Nasruddin opened the coffin, dragged Aslan's corpse to the river, and floated it out into the water. The current soon caught the lifeless body and carried it away.

That afternoon, the Mullah went here and there around the village, casually telling the people that Aslan was nearly qualified for sainthood. "This man was full of unknown merit. No doubt, he has raised his spirit from his coffin from inside the grave, and ascended into heaven."

Everyone believed Nasruddin and accepted his words of confidence. However, the next day, one of the villagers happened to spot a corpse that had washed up on the riverbank and called his neighbors. Once the authorities and everyone involved arrived, they examined the body and identified it as having been Aslan, the man they buried just the day before.

When the villagers checked the coffin and discovered it empty, they said, "Tomorrow we will go to the Mullah and reclaim the money for the funeral of this man, or at least a partial refund!"

The next day the group went to him and gave him the reasons for their objections in detail. Without hesitation, Nasruddin replied to that gullible group, "At first God took Aslan for a good and faithful man, but then God discovered that He had made a mistake. When God realized His awful mistake, He threw the poor soul back down from above."

TOUCHED BY HER HAND

Once, Nasruddin disguised himself with a veil and mingled undetected among some women who were gathered around a priest, questioning him about religious practice. One woman asked the cleric, "Is a prayer valid, even if we do not shave our pubic hair completely off?"

The priest replied, "If a woman's pubic hair is too long, it is shameful, and you must shave it; otherwise, it diminishes the validity of your prayer!"

Another woman asked, "How long may our pubic hair be grown before the prayer becomes invalid?"

The priest replied, "If it has reached the length of a single grain of barley, you must shave it!"

The disguised Nasruddin asked the woman standing next to him, "Sister, it has been a week or longer since last I shaved. Please check with your hand, to make sure that my pubic hair is not too long that it has reached this shameful length."

When the woman put her hand into his trousers and felt his cock, she shrieked. The priest said to Nasruddin, "Certainly, your piety has stirred her heart."

"No, you fool!" replied Nasruddin. "My Willie only touched her hand. You should hear how she would scream if he touched her heart."

COUNTING AND PULLING

Ahmet ran into the chai shop one morning in a panic. He pleaded, "Father, my friend, Abdul, is stuck on top of his house — please come and help him!"

Mullah and the men immediately left and followed the boy, who explained what happened as they ran. "Abdul was up there repainting their roof, and had just finished applying the final coat across the entire rooftop when he realized he had backed himself to the edge of the roof opposite to that of the stairs."

Nasruddin arrived to find Abdul, a husky boy, standing forlornly on the corner of the roof of his house.

Nobody had a ladder tall enough to reach the roof, and now Abdul was stuck. He could walk back across the roof to the stairs, leaving tracks in the paint that he'd have to repaint. Or he could jump, which would likely injure him. Or he could stay there until the paint dried, which might take the better part of the afternoon; or perhaps somehow Mullah could figure out how to get Abdul down.

Nasruddin stroked his white beard and said, "Well, I'm considering a course of action that was successful in another situation — I was able to save three men then, but I'm not so sure this method would work in this case. Still, I must do everything I can to try to rescue him."

He told Ahmet, "Bring me a long rope." While the boy ran to get the rope, the Mullah yelled up to Abdul, "Hang in there, child — I believe we have a solution at hand."

"Thank you," called out Abdul. "I'm starting to feel a bit dizzy."

When Ahmet returned, the Mullah directed the menfolk, "Come and line up behind me, holding onto the rope." The men arranged themselves, and Nasruddin tossed the other end of the rope to Abdul.

The Mullah said, "Tie the rope securely around your waist and make sure it's knotted tightly." Abdul did as instructed. Then Nasruddin spoke to the men lined up behind him, holding the rope, "All right now, grab the rope firmly, and on the count of three, pull together!"

Abdul said, "Wait! Are you quite certain this will work?"

"As I believe I mentioned already, I have used almost the exact same technique to rescue three men before. Trust me."

Nasruddin checked the line of men and called out, "One. Two. Three!"

Nasruddin and all the men jerked the rope hard and, finding hardly any resistance at the other end of the line, tumbled backward onto each other in a pile on the ground. Abdul was yanked off the roof, briefly seeming as if he were flying, but shortly his body plummeted straight down. From the crunch of his impact, it was apparent that the boy's landing had broken something.

"Ai vai! Big ass, big pain in the ass," Nasruddin said, as he rubbed his bruised backside. "Something went wrong. Virtually the same method had worked perfectly when I saved three guys who were stuck."

"What happened then?" Hamza said. "Where in the name of Allah did you save these people from, using this way of counting to three and pulling?"

"Well," Nasruddin replied sheepishly, "They had fallen in wells."

When they reached the boy, he was motionless on the ground. "What have you done?" asked Hamza. Nasruddin called for a doctor, and they brought Hamid.

"Dear God, Mullah," exclaimed Hamid, "this child is dead!"

"Why don't you tell me something I don't already know? I already figured that much out," replied Nasruddin. "But Hamid — look at the lad, do you see how his stomach is so swollen? I wonder, in your professional opinion, would you say he possibly could have been pregnant and had a little son of his own someday soon?"

GONE NUT

One cold, blustery morning, Nasruddin was relaxing in the hammam, the public bathhouse, for men. It was normally a leisurely, relaxing time for him to meditate on life while Mesut, the hammamji, poured bowl after bowl of steaming hot water over him.

In the middle of thoroughly enjoying his bath, he remembered that he had forgotten something — he had an appointment at noon to meet his friend Jalal who was traveling from Konya to Akşehir to visit for a few days. Not wanting to be absent if Jalal should arrive early, Nasruddin ran out of the steam room and quickly dressed while he was still wet.

When he stepped outside, the cold wind blew up through his legs, which made his scrotum shrink. Feeling something odd going on, he looked inside his baggy pants and discovered that one of his balls had disappeared.

Immediately he went back into the hammam and searched through the men present in the steam room, lifting their towels and staring between their legs while asking accusatorially, "Did you take my ball? Did you steal it?"

Mesut came up to him and said, "What the fuck's wrong with you, Mullah? Stop berating our customers."

Nasruddin complained, "One of my nuts has been stolen!"

"Impossible. Believe me, all these men have their own nuts."

"So it would seem! Well, I certainly didn't lose it on purpose."

"We have not found any extra balls. Where exactly did you see yours last?"

Nasruddin said, "Right here under my dick, next to his brother."

Mesut asserted, "In our many years running a respectable hammam, we have never lost an egg. Mullah, show me yours."

By now of course, because it was warm inside the hammam, Nasruddin's testicle had dropped. When the Mullah showed Mesut his crotch and they discovered his lost nut, he cried, "Everything that you can not steal by hand, finally comes back!"

FOUR-LEGGED DUCKS

Mullah Nasruddin was preaching in the mosque, and while he spoke, he became annoyed and then angry because he saw that some members of the congregation were yawning — some of them had even nodded off to sleep.

He paused, then began to talk loudly, "Yesterday, I was taking a stroll down by the river, when I happened to see four-legged ducks drinking coffee."

When the people heard the phrase "four-legged ducks," their eyes opened, their ears pricked up, and their jaws dropped. Now they began to listen very carefully to the Mullah.

This made him even angrier, yelling at the congregation, "Why are you here, Muslims? The whole time I'm giving a thoughtful and impassioned sermon about some aspect of the Truth, and every single one of you falls asleep. But the moment I pull a whopper of a lie out of my ass, you all awaken and pay rapt attention."

GOD'S DESIGN

One Sunday, Mullah Nasruddin mounted the pulpit and seized the Quran, preaching, "Oh Muslims, let us be ever thankful to God that he did not create us with our cock in the back."

Someone asked, "Why is that, Mullah?"

"People might accidentally screw themselves and therefore commit a sin before which the prophet of God, Lot, alone had kept for himself!"

A THREAT OF JUSTICE

One day when Nasruddin was serving as a judge, two men presented their case to him. The first fellow said, "Your Honor, I loaned this man fifty silver coins a year ago, and now he won't pay me back."

Nasruddin asked the accused man, "Is this correct?"

"No, your Honor," the fellow answered blankly.

The Mullah turned to the plaintiff and said, "You say that he owes you money. He says there is no debt. Whom am I to believe?""

"Excuse me, your Honor, but — by answering just once like this, would you take his word over mine and relieve his debt to me? How unfair is that?"

"Alrighty then, smartass," smirked the Mullah, "what do you recommend I do?"

"How should I know? You're the legal expert here. Do something to freak him out. Threaten or frighten him to do the right thing. Tell him that I'm not kidding and that this is not a joke. I want the fifty silver coins he took from me, and I want them back now!"

Nasruddin got down from the bench and approached the defendant. He put two fingers of both hands in his mouth to stretch out his lips, then used two more digits to pull back his eyelids. Walking ominously toward the second man with his face screwed up in this grotesque contortion, he screamed, "Hey, you fuckwad! I sure hope you're scared. Now pay back the money you borrowed from this man!" Any questions?"

NO HARM ON THE OUTSIDE

Tamerlane decided one day to test Nasruddin's nerve and obeisance. The tyrant ordered him to stand before the court, in front of a large wooden shooting target, with his arms spread wide open. "You are to stay there absolutely still, while three of my finest archers will each shoot a single arrow at you." Nasruddin complied, trying to look confident and brave, as he took place before the target and opened his arms wide.

The first archer stepped up, aimed quickly, and sent the arrow hurtling forward. The hissing shaft hit the mark with a *thhhhpp* just below his left wrist, pinning his shirtsleeve. As the court erupted in loud applause, Nasruddin showed a courageous face, silently reciting verses from the Quran that pertain to survival.

The second soldier walked up, aimed, and shot. The arrow sliced through the air and landed with an even louder *thwickkk* just below Nasruddin's right elbow. Now both his arms were immobilized, but still, he kept composed, fervently praying to Allah. The courtiers were highly amused, as the last archer stepped up and drew his bow.

With a juddering *thwappp*, the third arrow pierced the knot at the top of Nasruddin's turban, pinning it to the target behind him. For a moment everyone held their breath thinking at first that Nasruddin fainted, because his eyes were closed and he was motionless. At last, he opened his eyes and let out a small laugh.

Tamerlane cheered, "Well done, Nasruddin, you have passed my test! I commend your courageousness. Rest assured I will replace your shirt and turban with fine new garments, and reward you later. Congratulations!"

Nasruddin replied in a weak voice, "If it pleases your Majesty, I beg of you to issue me a set of trousers as well, so that I may have a complete set of new clothes."

"Of course, but your pants were not cut or damaged by an arrow."

"Quite true," said Nasruddin, "your archers did my trousers no harm on the outside. However, the inside of my trousers is a completely different situation."

WHY CAMELS ARE FLIGHTLESS

Nasruddin was preaching in Sivrihisar, when he declared, "Oh true believers! We must give thanks to Allah for His infinite wisdom. For example, thank God that He did not give the camel wings."

The congregation was confused. "Please explain, Mullah," Hussein said.

Nasruddin explained, "If He had, imagine what it would be like. Camels would be flying over our homes and shitting down the chimneys, not to mention that if they landed, they likely would come crashing through our roofs."

SILENT DOVE

Imad asked the Mullah, "After the great flood, the dove that brought the olive branch to the Prophet Noah — was it male or female?"

The Mullah replied, "Male, of course. If the bird had been female, she never could have kept her beak closed long enough to bring the branch back to Noah."

THIRD THIEF'S A CHARM

One day, three thieves broke into Mullah Nasruddin's house. They grabbed him and demanded, "Tell us where you hide your money."

Nasruddin denied having any cash hidden, but the crooks didn't believe him. "Until you confess the location of your treasure, you will stand on one leg."

So they made the Mullah stand on one leg. After several hours, the thieves became sleepy, so they decided to take turns keeping watch over Nasruddin. Two of the men fell asleep while the third stayed awake with Nasruddin, threatening him with a large knife from escaping.

Halfway through the night, the third thief felt a wave of compassion for the Mullah and whispered to him, "Okay, my friend, you can switch legs. Just don't tell the other guys."

Relieved, the Mullah thanked the third thief and told him quietly, "My son, you seem like a decent fellow. So I'll tell you this: my money is stashed in the backyard shed behind the mulberry tree. Without waking your friends, quickly go now and take the money all for yourself. Then scram and don't look back."

THE HAFIZ AND THE SLIPCASE

Once Mullah Nasruddin met a *hafiz*, someone who had memorized the Quran and was able to recite it from memory. Thinking Nasruddin for a chump, the hafiz attempted to assert his intellectual and moral ascendancy over the Mullah. He asked, "Tell me, Nasruddin, if you have two books together, whether any sort of book, or a copy of the Holy Quran, should be on top?"

Since it is common religious practice not to place anything on top of a copy of the Quran, the hafiz was suggesting that he was superior to the Mullah, because a hafiz only recites the holy Quran while a teacher like Nasruddin reads and recites books on general subjects.

Unwilling to let the hafiz get the upper hand, Nasruddin replied, "I would rather consider you to be like a slipcase of the Quran." So Nasruddin, while acknowledging that Quran is on top, implied that the hafiz was actually more like an empty case of the Quran, a shell that may be pleasant on the outside but is vacant within. Nasruddin's assertion was that indeed he is superior to the hafiz, just like any book is more respected than an empty book slipcase.

THE RIDDLE

One afternoon, Mullah posed this riddle to the chai shop wags: "Who has entered, come out, and will enter again; entered, come out, will not enter again; not yet entered, will enter; and not yet entered, and will never enter?"

Everyone was dumbfounded.

The Mullah said, "Here are the answers: Adam and Eve; Satan; the Muslims; and the infidels."

SHOCK TREATMENT

The King decided one day to put Nasruddin's wit to the test, so he summoned the Mullah and told him, "I have an intellectual challenge for you, Nasruddin. I want to see if you can shock or offend me, as a surprise, in a manner that your explanation will be turn out to be exponentially worse than the original effrontery."

"As you wish, your Majesty," he replied, exiting with a slight bow.

Several days later, the King and Nasruddin were strolling in the palace gardens discussing politics when, apropos of nothing, the Mullah grabbed the King by the beard, pulled him into a tight embrace, fondled the royal junk, and kissed him full on the mouth.

The astonished ruler broke off, spluttering, "What the fuck do you think you're doing, Nasruddin?"

Nasruddin slapped Tamerlane on the rump, then stepped back with a terrified look on his face. "Oh, please forgive me, your Majesty," exclaimed the Mullah. "For a moment there, I was confused and mistook you for your wife."

WHAT GOES UP

One day in the chai shop, Hussein asked Nasruddin, "Tell us, Mullah: is it possible for a vulva to fly?"

Nasruddin looked up heavenward and pulled down his pants, then stuck out his hard dick, curving right up. Then he said, "It doesn't matter. Just let it fly! Sooner or later, it will have to land on this."

GRAVE SITUATION

M esut, Luqman, and several other townsfolk considered themselves, at least for a while, to be Nasruddin's enemies. They wanted to get rid of him once and for all, and so they called together a group to form a lynch mob. Nasruddin overheard the men scheming, however, and learned that they planned to come in an hour to his house.

Nasruddin calmly went in his backyard with his spade and dug a narrow grave in the garden. Fatima went out to see what he was doing. "When my enemies come looking for me," Mullah instructed her, "tell them that I died from a horrible heart attack. When they ask for proof, just tell them if they want to pay their respects that my grave is in the garden and that you will lead them out back and show it to them, one at a time."

The Mullah went back out, took his old family branding iron and a small charcoal brazier and lay down in the grave, then he covered the pit with an old board that had a knothole about the size of a fist in the center.

Soon, Mesut and the band of Nasruddin's adversaries arrived and asked Fatima where her husband was.

"My poor husband is dead!" sobbed Fatima, and offered to show them the grave, one by one. The men were secretly delighted that God had already accomplished what they had been scheming for so long. Mesut quietly suggested to the group, "Let's all take a dump on him!" The men agreed that it was a splendid idea.

Fatima showed Mesut out to the backyard, then went back into the house. Mesut approached the grave, then pulled down his pants and squatted on Nasruddin's grave over the open hole.

Nasruddin, hidden in the grave, had heated the branding seal in the charcoal fire. When Mesut hovered over the hole, the Mullah stuck out the red-hot iron and burned Mesut's rump with it, branding him with the family seal.

Although Mesut wanted to yell out in pain, he controlled himself, not because he realized the Mullah had tricked him — but because he was hoping the same fate would eventually befall each of his wicked accomplices. So Mesut simply stood up, adjusted his trousers, and walked back in the house, where he informed Luqman that it was now his turn. One by one, they each came to be branded on their backsides, and the Nasruddin family seal marked them all.

Furious later that the Mullah had hoodwinked them yet once again, Mesut and the angry crowd went to the Sultan to complain that the Mullah had played a cruel hoax on them. Tamerlane called for the Mullah to be brought before him, and asked him to frankly explain how he came to have such a bad reputation among his townsmen.

Nasruddin defended himself, saying, "Everything that these men accuse me of is all resentment, lies, and deception, your Majesty! It is true, however, that these people who accuse me, every single one of them, are slaves of my father. If you do not believe me, you can inspect for yourself and see that each one of them has the family seal branded on his ass."

Tamerlane commanded the men to expose their backsides, and, of course, they discovered that Nasruddin's assertion was correct. So the sultan decreed that Mesut and the rest of Mullah's enemies were sentenced to serve their master for the rest of their lives.

SPECIAL CASH

When the Mullah was at the market one day, he noticed a man in the crowd counting his dinars very carefully.

The Mullah shouted out to the man, "What's so special about that money? Is it perhaps the cash that the money changer promised to your mother so she would fuck him?"

SOWING CAMEL SEEDS

One day in early spring, while Mullah Nasruddin was ploughing his barley field, his friends Hamza and Faruk came up to him and asked, "Mullah, what are you planting here?"

"Camel seeds," he answered. The Mullah then chatted with his friends for a few minutes before they continued on their way.

Some months later, Nasruddin was walking out to the field when he saw three camels munching on the barley growing there. He reined them and led the animals back to his stable, then went to the house and told Fatima, "My camel seeds have at last sprouted, seemingly overnight."

The next day, Musa, owner of the camels, finally noticed his animals had escaped their pen. Carefully, he followed their tracks to the Mullah's place. He knocked at the front door of the house.

When the Mullah answered the door, Musa said, "My camels ran off, and I followed them here. Please give them back to me."

Nasruddin scoffed, "What sort of bullshit is this? Those camels are the crop that I sowed in my own field."

Musa took Nasruddin to court. When Bekri, the judge, asked the Mullah to speak in his defense, he said, "Your Honor, those animals are the product of camel seeds I planted months ago."

Bekri asked him, "Do you have any evidence or witnesses?"

"I most certainly do have witnesses. Let me get them." Nasruddin left the court and brought Hamza and Faruk back before the judge.

Bekri asked them, "Did you witness the defendant, Nasruddin, planting camel seeds in his field?"

Faruk said, "Yes, it's true, we saw it. Early in the spring, we stopped by the Mullah's place and saw him sowing camel seed in his field." Hamza confirmed the facts.

There was nothing left for Musa to say, so the judge said, "I rule in favor of Nasruddin. Case dismissed."

TO EASE THE PAIN

Due to extenuating circumstances, Nasruddin happened to be in the company of two notorious thieves, Salim and Telal, when Luqman, the town watchman, apprehended and arrested them. Implicated in the thefts, the Mullah was brought with the others before Bekri, the judge, who ordered that all three men be whipped five times, but with a specific allowance: each man could request something to mitigate the sting of the whip on his back.

The first man to be whipped, a wiry scoundrel with dark hairy skin, Salim, requested oil to be put on his back before the whipping, and his wish was granted.

The next to be lashed, Telal, a barrel-chested rascal with bright smooth skin, stepped up and asked that honey be put on his back before the whipping was administered, and his request was granted as well.

Nasruddin stepped up and positioned himself, ready to be whipped. The whip-master stepped back and asked, "Nasruddin, what do you want us to place on your back to ease the nasty sting of my whip?"

"Since you asked," replied the Mullah, "here is my request. Before you crack the whip on me, please, I want Telal to sit on my back."

OX ATOP THE POLE

Nasruddin needed desperately to borrow money from his friend Jalal, who lived in Konya. Jalal knew that the Mullah and his money were soon parted, so he put the cash in a leather pouch for safekeeping and advised him to be extra cautious on the trip home.

Like most folks, Nasruddin worried about money a lot when he had none, and he worried about it even more when he had only a little. All the way back, Nasruddin felt fearful and paranoid, continually looking over his shoulder and clutching the purse to his chest. "Upon my return, I must find a safe place to hide this money," he resolved.

But by the time Nasruddin crossed the town square on his way home, he had not come up with a secure place, not even in his own home, where he could stash his cash.

As he approached the far edge of the square, he noticed a tall flagpole and thought, *Here's an obviously safe place — nobody would ever think to look up there for my money.* So he shimmied up the pole, left the money pouch dangling from the top, climbed down, and went home to recover from his journey, knowing his loan was secure.

As soon as Nasruddin left the square, some street urchins who had watched the whole scene ran to the pole. One climbed up, replaced the cash with an ox turd, and set the pouch back atop the pole exactly as Nasruddin left it.

The next day, when Nasruddin returned with Fatima to retrieve the money, he scaled the pole, grabbed the purse, and brought it down to the ground. When he opened the pouch, the turd fell out.

Nasruddin and Fatima stood there, astounded. Finally, Nasruddin exclaimed, "How in Allah's name did an ox get way up to the top of that pole?"

CAMELS AND MOUNTAIN TREES

One lovely spring morning, Nasruddin was in the mountain woods, high up in a tree, chopping down branches for firewood. As he was working, several men riding camels approached."

Nasruddin yelled, "Stop right there and don't come any closer! Don't any of you move an inch!"

The riders brought their camels to an abrupt halt, nearly spooking them. The Mullah put his fingers to his lips, indicating he wanted silence. After everyone was still and quiet for a seemingly endless minute, Nasruddin descended the tree. On the ground, he said, "Okay now, you can come through."

Annoyed at the disruption in their travels, the camel riders resumed their pace. Their leader asked, "Why in Allah's name did you make us stop our camels?"

"You dumb sonofabitch," sneered Nasruddin, "we never get camels up here in the mountains. Can't you see that these are mountain trees? Your ignorant camels probably have never seen such a thing, and they might have been frightened by it and knocked it to the ground while I was up there."

A FRIEND'S SUPPORT

When Hussein, one of Nasruddin's oldest and dearest friends, passed away, the Mullah was inconsolable. He slowly followed the funeral procession, constantly sobbing and beating his chest in great sorrow, "Who will now take an oath to me, if I should lie? Who will now urge me to drink wine, even if I should feel remorse? And who will now pay for me in a brothel, if I have no money?"

The Mullah cried, "May Allah, after the death of my longtime conspirator, never mislead me! Ai vai! If only He had not deprived me of my dear friend's support!"

LOST AND FOUND LEGS

One warm afternoon, Mullah Nasruddin was nodding off in a peaceful day-dream as he rode his faithful little gray donkey Karakacan (backward, as was his habit) past Lake Akşehir on his usual return trip home.

The local boys swimming in the lake, knowing the Mullah would pass nearby, had decided to try to play another one of their pranks on Nasruddin.

The Mullah's students were always thinking up ways to fool their beloved teacher, even though nine out of ten tricks ended up backfiring on them. Still, loving fresh mischief just as much as kids nowadays, the boys delighted in coming up with new antics and challenges.

Quickly they huddled together knee-deep in the shallow water of the brook, legs locked and stiff as if their feet had taken root in the muddy bottom of the lake.

They heard the steady, slow, familiar clip-clop of Karakacan's hooves on the ground as the Mullah approached.

"Should we call out to him?" whispered Mehmet.

"He always addresses us first," hissed back Ishmail, who had his back turned to the bank. "If we stand here as if we're stuck in the mud and wait for him to speak first, he won't suspect anything."

The sound of donkey hooves slowed, then stopped close to the boys. There was a long silence before the Mullah spoke.

"Good morning, boys!" said Nasruddin. "What do you see in that dark water that makes you stand together like young bamboo trees?"

"Mullah! Allah be praised that you have heard our prayers!" called out Ishmail over his shoulder. "Ai vai! Help us! We are stuck!"

"What seems to be the problem, children?"

"When we arrived here at the brook, each boy had his own legs," whined Mehmet. The boys seemed to strain at pulling their legs out of the water, and indeed, they appeared to be stuck in the mud. "

Ishmail said, "But we have been swimming so long now that all our legs are mixed up. Please — you must help us sort out which legs are which!"

"Which legs are whose," replied Nasruddin, ever the pedant, drowsily dismounting his donkey.

At first, the situation indeed looked confounding. Mehmet's right leg was paired up with Ishmail's left foot and Abdul's right foot. Ishmail's right leg and Sedat's right leg had somehow joined together with Nuri's torso. Nuri's right foot was still unaccounted for.

As the boys implored Nasruddin to come in — they were only six or seven feet out in the water — to save them from their horrible fate, he stroked his long white beard and clucked his tongue as if he might be very sorry for the boys — or it may have meant something else entirely.

After considering the situation for several minutes, he went to the saddlebag on his donkey and pulled out a small ax, with which he chopped off a supple branch about nine feet long from a nearby tree. He then proceeded to trim all the excess leaves and offshoots from the main branch.

"Here, this should fix your dilemma," said Nasruddin, returning to the edge of the water with the switch, which he started to wield most effectively on the backs, legs, arms, and shoulders of the boys.

The boys who could see Nasruddin were able to duck the lashes, but Ishmail, being closest with his back to Nasruddin, ended up getting the brunt of Mullah's solution for mixed-up legs. Finally Ishmail could stand the abuse no more and jumped up howling, scattering the circle of boys.

"There you go," said Nasruddin, "you found your own legs, after all, without my help."

Without a stitch of his clothing wet, Nasruddin threw the switch in the water, then mounted Karakacan. As he rode away backward, watching the boys as they scrambled up the bank to inspect their welts, he waved and called out, "You boys better hang onto that stick — just in case your legs should happen to get all screwed up again."

CAREFUL EXECUTION

In Tamerlane's court one day, Nasruddin pulled the tyrant's beard, made fun of his first wife, and told a crude joke about his lame leg that insulted him, and so the Sultan called for his head. Promptly, a bearish leather-clad executioner wearing a black hood and carrying a large scimitar appeared.

As the executioner approached him, smirking and swinging his ax, the Mullah raised his head, cleared his throat, and said, "Sir, please take care that your big sword doesn't chip the cupping-glass on my neck."

Cupping is an ancient healing technique using hollow glass spheres, warmed and applied in places where disease is suspected, that when cooling creates a vacuum adhering the cups to the skin, thus increasing topical circulation.

The burly executioner paused and snarled, "You poor fool, you are about to meet your destiny. Why should I listen to anything you have to say?"

The Mullah explained, "But sir, you see, I'm under the longterm care of a physician who is a master in the therapeutic practice of cupping. Just this morning, I had a healing treatment with him, and one of his cups is still on the neck you intend to sever from the rest of my body."

"So what?" spat the axman. "Well, bloody lovely for you that you're feeling chipper today. Now prepare to die." He raised his weapon, ready to lop off Nasruddin's head.

Nasruddin pleaded, "But . . . but I have another appointment tomorrow and would really like to return the cup to him, undamaged."

Before the executioner could bring down his sword, the Sultan laughed at this outrageous response and halted the beheading. After giving the Mullah a reward for his audacity, he set him free.

REPARATIONS

One time when Mullah Nasruddin was a judge, a man and a woman appeared before the high court.

The woman said, "Your Honor, this man is not an acquaintance of mine. I was standing in the town square, minding my own business, and suddenly he grabbed me and kissed me. I want reparations for that. I am entitled to justice."

"Certainly you are entitled to compensation, my daughter," said the Mullah. "So in my judgment, it's only fair that now you should turn toward him, grab him, and kiss him, just as he did to you. There, now you're even."

WHY THE SKY HAS NO POLES

One day as Nasruddin was preaching on the rostrum, he declared, "Oh true believers! We must give thanks to Allah for His infinite wisdom. For example, praise be to God that He created the sky without poles."

The congregation was confused.

Nasruddin explained, "If He had, imagine what it would be like. To make a pole stand sturdy enough to hold up the entire sky, all the trees and rocks in the world would not be sufficient."

TURBAN DOUBLES AS CUSHION

Mullah Nasruddin was invited by his student Imad's parents to join their family for Ramadan dinner. To start the meal, he was served boiling, spicy pepper soup. The Mullah took a spoonful of the soup and put it to his mouth, but once he tasted it, he dared not return the spoon to his plate and risk having to choke any more of it down.

Then he removed his turban from his bald head, put it on his chair, and sat on it. The host asked Nasruddin, "Why is it you're sitting on your cap?"

The Mullah replied, "I did not want the fire burning in my stomach to spread down on to your beautiful seat covers. Since the turban is mine, there will be no harm done when it burns through."

A NASTY FELLOW

When Mullah Nasruddin was elderly, he used a walking stick to help him get around. One day, Faruk, one of Mullah's neighbors, decided to play a nasty trick on him and broke his cane. Nasruddin was furious and cursed him, saying, "That cane was like my right arm! Damn you, Faruk! Allah is on my side, and He will avenge me, Before forty days have passed, you will break your leg."

Faruk looked at the Mullah and laughed in derision. Faruk walked away, not paying attention to where he was stepping, tripped over a stone, fell, and broke his leg. He hobbled over to the Mullah and cried out in pain, "Nasruddin, you cursed to make me to break my leg in forty days — but only minutes have passed and I've already injured it!"

"Serves you right — and in the next forty days, or less, you'll break the other leg, and then you'll have to crawl on your hands and belly."

FOLLOW THE LEADER

Nasruddin walked to the mosque and, as is customary, he left his pointy shoes outside, went inside, and sat down cross-legged in the first row, right in front of the imam.

As the mosque filled, Mullah's neighbor Hussein was seated in the row behind him. As they bowed in unison during the *namaz*, Hussein couldn't help but notice that Nasruddin's shirttail was rather short and, each time Nasruddin kneeled forward, he exposed his junk.

Hussein, thinking it looked unseemly, was affronted by the spectacle. *I did not come here to the mosque to pray,* he thought, *to have revealed to me a vision of Nasruddin's hairy ass and balls.* So he reached out and tugged Nasruddin's balls before pulling down the shirttail to let him know that they were exposed, and then he proceeded with his namaz.

Immediately Nasruddin leaned forward and yanked on the balls of the man in front of him, the imam, who was naturally quite startled.

The imam said, "What in the name of Allah are you doing?"

Nasruddin shrugged and pointed his thumb behind him at Hussein, saying, "Don't ask me — ask the fellow behind me — he started it. I thought we were playing mutual egg goosing."

God's Arrears to Nasruddin

Times were tough. The economy was in the pits, and unemployment was sky-rocketing. "I cannot find a job," declared Nasruddin one day to his wife, "as I am already employed full time in the service of the All-Highest."

"In that case," suggested Fatima, "you should ask for your back wages because every employer must pay."

"That makes uncommon sense," said the Mullah. "Perhaps I have never been paid because I have never bothered to request a fee."

"Then you had better go right this minute and ask," said Fatima.

Nasruddin entered the garden, knelt on a prayer mat, and cried out in supplication, "Oh Allah, this is your devoted servant Nasruddin here. Send me exactly one hundred — no fewer or more, please — gold coins, for all my past services are worth precisely that much."

Aslan, a wealthy Jewish merchant whose yard adjoined the Nasruddin household, overheard the Mullah's plaintive demands for payment of overdue wages owed and thought he'd teach his needy, beleaguered neighbor what he considered a long overdue lesson.

While Nasruddin continued praying to Allah for his salary in the exact amount of one hundred gold coins, Aslan quickly crept up to his private chambers, where he kept his money. The Jew counted out precisely ninety-nine gold coins, put them into a bag, and tied the sack closed. Then he quietly stepped out onto the roof of his house.

Just as Nasruddin's head was bent to the ground, Aslan threw the bag from his window into the next yard and quickly crept down from the roof to stand at the latticed window in his wife's room, where he could observe his neighbor's reaction undetected.

The bag had knocked the turban right off Nasruddin's balding head, landing with a soft clinking thud onto his prayer rug. The Mullah gasped in surprise, then looked skyward in curious and hopeful anticipation.

Without offering so much as a word of thanks to Allah, Nasruddin emptied the sack onto his prayer rug and counted the coins, then recounted them, and recounted them again. He couldn't seem to believe the result he was getting.

Aslan had to stifle his laughter at Nasruddin's puzzlement as he crept away from the window, thinking that he'd keep poor old Nasruddin in the dark for a couple days before he let him in on the joke.

Finally, Nasruddin announced, "You can owe me the last one." He put the coins back in its bag, rolled up his prayer rug, and took his newfound earnings inside.

Nasruddin sat down across from Fatima, then said, "I am one of the saints." He tossed the bag of gold coins on the table, saying, "Here are my arrears." She was indeed quite impressed.

The next day, Aslan, suspicious at the succession of deliveries of food and furnishings to Nasruddin's front gate, went next door to explain the prank he had pulled and to declare that the ninety-nine gold coins were his.

Nasruddin said, "You must have heard me calling for my fee, and now you pretend that the money is yours. You shall never have it, as my payday from God has been long overdue."

Aslan said, "You greedy thief! Then we must immediately go to the court of summary jurisdiction to have the regional judge settle this dispute."

"Don't be ridiculous. I cannot go looking like this. I have a rip in my cloak that Fatima has to mend. If you sue me and we appear in court together, and you are dressed so much better than me, undoubtedly the magistrate will be prejudiced in your favor."

"All right," Aslan said, "Fair enough. I'll lend you a proper robe you can wear to court."

"Also, my donkey's leg is lame," Nasruddin informed his neighbor, "and so I'll also need to borrow a horse, saddle, and bridle, if you don't mind." Impatiently, Aslan got Nasruddin suitably mounted onto one of his own horses, and the two men rode to court.

Aslan brought his suit to court before Bekri, the judge, "The ninety-nine gold coins in Nasruddin's possession are mine, your honor."

Nasruddin asked to approach the bench, then pleaded his case calmly, whispering to the judge, "Your esteemed Honor, with your superior intelligence you can tell that this neighbor of mine is clearly bonkers. For some strange reason, he thinks everything of mine is automatically his."

"That's quite a counterclaim," said Bekri. "What evidence of this do you have, Nasruddin?"

"His very own words will betray him," Nasruddin asserted. "Not only does he claim that my gold is his, but he also will state that even this cloak is his."

"I object, your Honor. That robe is indeed mine!"

Nasruddin leaned in even closer, saying, "It's really quite pathological. Now, watch this rascal, next he will say that my horse is his, as well."

"But, your Honor! That is my horse!"

"Pitiful, pained, and petty," Nasruddin continued, "you can see how dissociated from reality he is. Listen, your Honor: next thing you know, he will claim that even my horse's bridle is his."

"B-but that bridle is mine as well!" stuttered Aslan, who fell to his knees and broke down into disconsolate sobbing.

"Order in the court!" called the judge, banging his gavel. "I rule in favor of Nasruddin. Case dismissed. Take this one away," Bekri declared, pointing to the forlorn Jew.

They hauled Aslan out of court by his beard and gave him a good thrashing. And the Mullah was allowed to return home with the cloak and the horse, and to keep the nine hundred and ninety-nine pieces of gold, which he had rightfully earned.

PART VII

Travels with the Mullah

THE SILK BROCADE

Once in Tamerlane's court, Mullah Nasruddin won his favor and received as a gift an exquisite silk brocade cloth. On the way back home, Nasruddin became quite parched. He came to an elegant house of a merchant named Jafar, and sat on the doorstep to wait if someone would come out of the house who could give him something to drink.

The merchant's wife, Ina, looking down through the slats in her shuttered casement, noticed the Mullah and his brocade. As he sat, he raised his head and saw a young woman, as radiant as the bright moon, looking at him curiously from her balcony. She called to him, "Mullah, what is it you want?"

"I have come from seeing Tamerlane in court, and I'm heading home. I would like a drink of water," Nasruddin replied. "But truly, I am searching for a lady who will accept this silk brocade — in exchange for letting me screw her."

Ina scolded him for being so forward but, at the same time, the gorgeous fabric captivated her. She asked her maidservant, Iesha, "How can we snatch that fabulous brocade without complying with his request?"

The servant replied, "What harm is it to anyone if we take the cloth from him and let him sleep with one of the slave girls? He's moronic and won't care about the difference. No one will know what he has done." So Ina ordered the maid to bring the Mullah in the kitchen.

As Iesha gave him some water, Ina came downstairs and instructed him to choose one of the servant girls. He refused, insisting, "I want none other than you."

She sniggered, "Your clothes are filthy, and you stink of grease. However, if you lie down, I will climb on top of you and satisfy your desire."

Ina mounted Nasruddin and rode him like a donkey. Just as soon as he came and she rolled off, he grabbed the silk brocade and stood up to leave. She said to him, "Where do you think you're going with that? It's mine now."

He retorted, "I'm taking *my* brocade back home with me. This fabric was given to me personally from Tamerlane. If he asks me about his gift — and we know that he will — I'll have to tell him you took it from me. Then both you and I will suffer the consequences." With Ina in hot pursuit, he tried to exit; however, Iesha stood in his way and wrested the cloth from his hands.

Nasruddin shouted, "By God and our King! These fiendish females would cheat me! They would rob me of my precious brocade!"

Iesha said, "You liar — you bargained and sold it for sex. I heard you!"

Nasruddin protested to Ina, "You denied me true satifaction because you insisted on being on top. Just look at me." He pointed to his still-strong desire. "You must let me fulfill my need with you." And so she agreed.

When he had satisfied his desire anew, once again he reached out and swiped the silk brocade. Ina yelled, "Nasruddin! What do you think you're doing?"

He said, "The second time, when I was lying on top of you, was to make up for the first time when *you* were on top. Now that we are even, I am simply taking back my original investment."

And so they argued back and forth until they finally came together a third time to resolve the issue once and for all; this time, the brocade stayed, and the Mullah went away.

The next afternoon, Nasruddin came to Jafar's door and asked Ina for a cup of water. She handed it to him and slammed the door shut. He drank it and dropped the ceramic so that it broke and shattered in every direction on the ground.

The Mullah sat down on the doorstep, with tears falling down his cheeks, when suddenly Jafar, the master of the house, came home. Ina stuck her head out of the window. He looked at her, and looked at Nasruddin and asked, "Good Mullah, what are you doing here?"

Nasruddin said, "I came here to ask for some water. As I drank, the cup fell out of my hand and broke. I had a precious brocade given to me by Tamerlane, which the mistress of the house snatched from me as compensation. I was waiting for you, effendi, to return, so that you might help me to recover my silk cloth."

Jafar looked up at Ina and asked her, "Was that how it happened?"

She said, "Well, not exactly — the Mullah is perhaps a bit confused . . ."

Nasruddin interjected, "Jafar, even though I may have missed a detail here or there, I have already explained to you basically what happened in my folly. Go now to the kitchen and see the broken pieces of the cup still there." Nasruddin turned to Ina and said, "So now you tell your version!" But she kept her eyes lowered and her mouth shut.

Naturally, Jafar gave Nasruddin back his silk brocade. Thus the Mullah had complete success with his guile.

What fits the minaret

Once Nasruddin was traveling in a strange town and came across an unusually tall minaret that he had never seen before. He asked one of the locals, "What is that? A deep well that has been turned inside out?"

The fellow replied, "Not at all. That's just a replica of the average-sized cocks of the men here."

"Really. If that's the case," declared Mullah, "I'd like to see the corresponding butthole to which it fits." Then he circled the minaret and asked, "Besides, where are the balls?"

Protection

Mullah Nasruddin went one afternoon to the public bathhouse, where the hammamji, Mesut, had long resented Nasruddin, mostly because the Mullah was not quite the best tipper in town, and because Mesut despised mullahs in general. As the attendant walked near Nasruddin, he deliberately bumped into him hard, almost shoving him. In reaction, Nasruddin grabbed his testicles.

Mesut snorted, "What's your problem, Mullah?"

"Oh, no problem at all!" he replied, "I have just grabbed my boys so that they will not drop down and get in your way. I certainly wouldn't want you to step on them by accident."

So many pimps

One day Mullah Nasruddin was traveling when he came across a bevy of women who were walking in rows, with one young woman in white in the lead. As the group passed by, he asked one of them what they were doing.

She answered him, "We're escorting a lovely young virgin girl to her wedding. Tonight, the newly wed wife and her husband, surrounded by all these women, will satisfy their desires."

"Allah save me!" cried the Mullah. "I am much traveled, but never have I been in a place where there are so many pimps!"

ONE ON EACH SIDE

Nasruddin was traveling to Konya when on the road he met five affable fellows, spiritual comrades who somehow reminded the Mullah of himself. They seemed friendly and interested in his teachings, so they traveled together for a while.

After a few hours, the men got hungry. As the hour was late, their hunger began to gnaw at them, and one of the Mullah's new followers asked, "Nasruddin, you are our leader on this journey, so tell us: what shall we feed ourselves? There is nothing here that we can eat."

The Mullah replied, "Hold on a moment. First, we ought to collect some firewood; then we will find something like a hare or something we can roast over the fire and then eat."

They were out in the country, and his new friends asked him, "Really? You think we can catch a rabbit?"

He said, "Sure, just a rabbit, a bird, a chicken. We will hunt it down, or as a last resort, we shall steal it from a farm. But first, let us gather kindling and wood together for the fire."

The friends agreed, "Well, let's wait as he suggests and collect the wood first, then we'll find some food to cook." They had no axes or other tools to help in the process, and so the men had to collect the wood by hand.

"I know an expedient method to gather wood, the Mullah proceeded to climb up a tall oak tree. He made it to a large upper branch and shouted down to his new disciples to follow him. The first man went up the tree and Nasruddin told him to hang onto his feet. Then he directed the second man to hang on to the legs of the first, and to the next man to do the same, and likewise with the other two.

Finally, after they all had formed a chain hanging from Nasruddin's legs, he called down to the men from the uppermost branch, "Well, guys — are you all ready? On my count of three, we'll pull down this branch, and then we can start a fire and make a nice dinner."

When the men answered in the affirmative, the Mullah said, "Just a second, brothers — I want to get a better grip! Hang on!" He let go of the branch to spit in his hands, and all the men fell one atop another in a pile.

On the ground, they discovered that only Nasruddin and the fellow right below him, Ozgur, were unhurt; all of the others were either maimed or wounded. So since only the Mullah and one man, Hamid, could walk, the two beat a hasty retreat and continued on their journey.

Finally, they arrived in a town where they saw a young man selling seeds in a bag, and Nasruddin asked him, "What are you vending in that bag?"

The seller replied, "These are nail seedlings."

"What are you saying? Nail seedlings? I've never heard of such a marvelous thing!" Nasruddin turned to his companion and asked, "Shall we buy some?"

"Yes," Ozgur agreed, "let us buy some and plant them."

The Mullah turned back to the vendor and asked, "Kindly sell us some of your precious seedlings."

"Yes, certainly. I will be only too happy to do so."

So with the few coins they had, they bought some of these nail seedlings.

The seller warned the men, "Do take extra care when you plant them, that the insects do not eat them!"

The Mullah assured the boy, "Don't worry. That's our concern, not yours."

Nasruddin and Hamid found some arable soil and planted the seedlings. Then they both kept a vigil, one on either side, to guard the seedlings, with a bow and arrow.

Now, there were some grasshoppers around who seemed to like this kind of seed. As the two men stood guard, side by side, weapon in hand, suddenly a grasshopper jumped right onto Ozgur's forehead.

The fellow quietly whistled to Nasruddin and pointed to indicate that the grasshopper had landed on his brow. Nasruddin watched, nodded, then carefully aimed his arrow and shot. Hitting his target, he killed the locust, but of course, also his friend. Stroking his beard, he remarked to the grasshopper, "Fair enough. One of our men, and one of yours."

WHY THEY PLUGGED IT UP

One day the Mullah was traveling and came to an unfamiliar town tired and thirsty. He noticed that close to the road there was a well, near which was a short standing water pipe, sealed with a plug. He said to himself, "Here is where I can drink some water." So he put his mouth right in front of the opening of the pipe and yanked the plug.

No sooner had he pulled it that the water gushed forth, knocking Nasruddin on his ass and soaking him from top to bottom. The Mullah walked over to the well. Pointing to the hydrant, he angrily shouted down the well, "Now I get it! Because you piss forth water so recklessly, they plugged your ass with a stopper!"

SHOULD KNOW BETTER

Once, Mullah Nasruddin traveled to the city of Malatya in central Turkey, and while he was walking along he noticed a little boy holding a piece of gold, turning it over in his hand.

Nasruddin said, "Say, boy, what are you doing with that counterfeit coin? Hand it to me, and I will give you a dinar for it."

The boy said, "Forget it, Mullah. I don't want your lousy dinar. What I want is for you to bray like a donkey. If you do that, I will give you this counterfeit coin."

So the Mullah got down on all fours and began to bray and bray, until finally the boy held up his hand and said, "Enough, you moron. If a fake donkey like you believes that this is a worthless slug, shouldn't a smart kid like me know that this is a piece of gold?"

FROM TEACHER TO NOVICE

In the chai shop one day, Faruk jokingly informed the Mullah, "I have heard that your last donkey has now become a judge in Konya!"

Nasruddin was thrilled at his family's turn of fortune and rushed home to tell Fatima, "Great news, my dear! Our little donkey has become a judge! I think I'll go see him and ask if he can give me a job as an assistant!"

The next morning, he set out on the road. At night he stayed at an inn and told the innkeeper's wife, "Kindly wake me before dawn. I have something important to accomplish in Konya early in the morning and must leave before sunrise!"

Also staying in the guesthouse were some students who noticed the Mullah. As a prank, while he slept, the boys silently shaved off his beard and mustache.

Early that morning, the hostess knocked on the door and shouted to the Mullah, "Hey you! Get up! It's almost dawn, and you must get going!" Nasruddin arose groggily and left the inn.

He trudged along the road for several hours, and after the sun had risen, he passed a spring and decided to rest there. When he leaned over a pool of water to scoop up a handful to drink, he noticed his reflection. He was shocked to see, not the grizzled beard of an aging mullah, but the shaven face of a novice monk!

After considering the matter for a while, he finally figured it out and slapped his forehead. "That fucking bitch at the inn was supposed to have awakened me, the Mullah — but instead she has woken up one of those ugly, stupid novices!"

SEMINAL EVIDENCE

Nasruddin was traveling with a group of men and several boys, and they camped for the night.

After everyone else in the large, pitch-black tent had fallen asleep, Nasruddin got up silently and busied himself on a boy. After Nasruddin shot his load on the kid's backside, he quickly, quietly retreated to his cot in a corner of the tent and pretended to be asleep.

The boy awoke a moment later and felt that his ass was wet and covered with semen. He immediately cried out and woke several of the men nearby with his sobs. The men lit a lamp and asked the boy what was going on, and he showed them the spunk dribbling down his legs.

One fellow said, "I know how we can find out who did this. Come, let us put our hands on the chests of all the sleeping men. The one whose heart beats fast — that's our man!"

Nasruddin heard this and rolled over onto his stomach, pulled up his robe to cover his head and to expose his backside, and smeared the slobber on his butt. Then he laid down and pretended to be asleep.

When the men came to Nasruddin, they saw that his buttocks were covered with globs of milky goo and said, "The last fellow here with the ass as hairy as a donkey — poor fellow, he too has already gotten fucked from behind!" And so they left him alone.

RECYCLING

After Nasruddin had cheated the whole world, he eventually came to Shkodër in Albania. Here, too, he wanted to start with his usual clever pranks. But in Shkodër, he encountered someone superior to him.

On a street near the bazaar entrance, he came across a boy who looked intelligent. The Mullah asked him, "You, child, tell me: what I can buy in Shkodër cheap, eat here, and then sell it again?"

"As much as you want, sir," replied the boy. "Just go to the butcher and buy yourself an animal intestine filled with crap. Then after you eat the contents of the intestine, you can then fill it with your own crap and sell it for as much as you bought it."

OFF MARKET

Penniless, Nasruddin was traveling in a strange city. Though he couldn't buy anything, he wandered around an open bazaar. He noticed, seated in an otherwise empty stall, a voluptuous woman, made up and dressed suggestively. He approached her and asked, "Lady, what are you selling?"

She replied, "What I wear on my back."

"I see," he said. "So will you then buy my cock?"

The woman said, "Sir, you are either incredibly stupid or crazy, or both."

The Mullah calmly said, "Believe me, if you don't want to either buy a dick or sell your pussy, then you have no business being here in this market."

AN INCONVENIENT TRUTH

One day, Nasruddin was traveling on pilgrimage when he came to a strange town, where he decided to stop for a drink of water. At the public well, he encountered a woman standing there to fetch water, who asked him, "Tell me, Mullah: why did you abandon your village?"

"I did not leave voluntarily. Because of my sincerity, and because I always speak the truth, the townspeople expelled me."

The woman shrugged. She bade the Mullah, "Come, help me. Please load these water bags on my shoulders."

The Mullah lifted the bags onto the woman's shoulders, then he stuck his hand between her legs and said, "If you don't mind, and if I'm not lying, then I believe that here is a safe place to stick my cock."

Gasped the woman, "So that was your way of telling your neighbors the truth."

AN EXCELLENT REMEDY

While Mullah Nasruddin was traveling, he was famished as he entered the city. When asked at the city gate of his profession, he replied, "I'm a doctor."

"If you're a physician, then you must come with us. We want to take you to heal the King's son, who is sick unto death." Nasruddin readily agreed.

So they brought him to the King's palace, who escorted him to the child's bedside. The royal inquired, "His condition is critical. What course of treatment or medicine do you prescribe for my son?"

"Tell me, do you have here in your house, the following ingredients: bread, butter, honey, and milk?"

"Yes, of course, we have all these things here."

"Then bring them all to me," asked the Mullah. "I'll start with the medical incantation and then produce an excellent remedy." Then he closed his eyes and began to mumble an unintelligible chant. They went to the pantry and brought Nasruddin everything he requested.

The Mullah mixed the butter with the honey and spread it on the bread; then he proceeded to eat the food and drink the glass of milk. The sovereign assumed this was all to test the effectiveness of this powerful remedy.

Soon the food and drink were gone and Nasruddin belched. Then the King exclaimed, "Doctor, what are you doing? My child has died while you were eating!"

Nasruddin only replied, "That is unfortunate, but had I not eaten the food right then, doubtlessly we both would have perished."

THE HOSPITALITY BOWL

Once, Nasruddin was traveling and entered a village that had a reputation for being inhospitable. The Mullah intended to test this stereotype, so he went up to the front door of a modest home and knocked. When the master of the house answered the knock, the Mullah requested a drink of water.

A moment later, the man reappeared at the door with a ceramic bowl full of milk. Nasruddin accepted it gratefully and drank it while the man watched, smiling sheepishly.

After thanking the fellow for his kindness, Nasruddin added, "You know, I'd heard that people in your town here were all stingy, unfriendly folk. I've found you, however, to be welcoming and generous. You didn't just offer me water: you gave me milk to drink."

"Well, normally I wouldn't have offered the milk," replied the man, "except that a mouse had fallen in the milk pail, so I poured it into this bowl for you."

Mullah, stunned at the betrayal, dropped the dish.

"Be careful, you fool!" yelled the man. "Don't break that bowl — it's the one that my daughter uses to piss in."

BACK ENTRANCE

M ullah Nasruddin was very proud and never bowed his head before any of the mighty leaders of the earth. Even when he saluted his superiors, he never lowered his head.

This pride angered the Pasha, who decided to trick the Nasruddin and force him into bowing before him.

To that end, he invited Nasruddin to his palace at Shkodër. At the front, in the foyer, he had a small door built, through which everyone had to duck their heads in order to pass through the entrance to the courtyard.

When Nasruddin arrived, in the foyer he approached the short doorway. The Pasha stood on the other side, eagerly awaiting the moment when the Mullah would emerge from the low door, finally, with his head bowed humbly before him.

But Nasruddin saw the new entrance and understood the situation. Turning himself around, he stuck his butt far out and walked backward through the doorway, much to the displeasure of the Pasha, who had expected some show of reverence and instead was greeted by a view of the Mullah's backside.

GOD OF THE EARTH

W hen Mullah Nasruddin was to meet Tamerlane for the first time, the conqueror said to his minister, "I must destroy Nasruddin. So I'll pose him some tough questions., and if he does not correctly answer even one of them, I'll have him promptly executed."

When the Mullah arrived, Tamerlane asked, "Who do you think you are?"

Nasruddin replied, "I am the god in charge of the earth!"

Well, Tamerlane was indeed a Tatar, meaning that he had a liking for young male companions. His attendant, standing by his side, was the most beautiful boy of his tribe, whose eyes, as it so happened, were quite small. Tamerlane said, "So, god of the earth! Look here at this beautiful boy! What do you say about him?"

"I've looked at him," said the Mullah. "But in all honesty — with his little eyes, he lacks a certain charm."

" 'But with his little eyes, he lacks a certain charm!' " Tamerlane mocked. "Since you are such a powerful god, or so you say, give me the pleasure of enlarging his eyes!"

Nasruddin replied coolly, "My lord, I am merely the god of the earth and am capable merely of widening an opening located below the waist. For openings above the waist, you must ask the god in charge of heaven, for he is responsible for those matters and I cannot interfere with his work."

A grin broke across Tamerlane's face.

"If your boy has a lower opening that needs widening, I would be only too happy to comply."

Timur laughed heartily at this reply, and declared, "Since you are such an endearing rascal, I swear that I never will be separated from you."

Nasruddin affirmed, "It is so, for you are my liege."

GOLD OR PEBBLES

Once, Mullah Nasruddin was traveling and arrived in a city where many of the roofs of the houses had flags on them. The Mullah was curious about the meaning of the flags.

Finally, he asked a local person, who informed him, "In our city, it is the custom that people who have a jarful of gold should place it on their roofs and plant a small flag in it."

The Mullah found the city charming and hospitable, so he decided to stay there for a while. One day, he bought several jars. Upon arriving back at his place, he filled the pots with pebbles he collected from the street and took them to the roof. He lined the containers along the edge of the roof and placed a flag into each one, just as he'd seen everyone else do.

But part of this quaint local custom Nasruddin had not been told. During a holiday, all the owners of the gold-filled jars gave parties for one another, during which they opened their jars and revealed the contents to their friends.

Nasruddin enjoyed this new custom very much, but eventually it was his turn to host a party. At the end of the feast, the guests were curious to see the Mullah's pots. They climbed up to the roof to see them, and when Nasruddin opened the pots, everyone saw that his jars were all filled with pebbles, not gold. "Hey Mullah, what's the meaning of this fraud?" someone asked. "Where is the gold? There's nothing but stones in all these jars."

Nasruddin shrugged and replied, "Since the jars are covered and idle, what difference in the least does it make what might be inside them?"

KILL THEM WHILE THEY'RE LITTLE

While traveling on the way to visit his friend Jalal in Konya, Mullah Nasruddin found himself walking peacefully along an unusual kind of roadway when he heard a shrill sound coming from behind. Nasruddin turned around and saw a huge black metal monster approaching, making a loud whistling noise and billowing steam from its chimney.

Thinking the monster rolling down the tracks right toward him was some sort of demon or deity, Nasruddin bowed down before it in supplication. Thankfully, before the beast could hit him, Nasruddin jumped out of its way just in time as it barreled its way down the tracks past him without slowing down in the least. Although Nasruddin was bruised and scratched up a bit, his injuries could have been much worse.

At long last, Nasruddin made it to Jalal's house, where he was welcomed and made comfortable. After the Mullah was all settled in, his host offered to make them a pot of tea, so he put a water kettle on the stove. After a few minutes, the teakettle started to whistle, and then spouted steam.

Trembling with fear, Nasruddin jumped up from his seat, grabbed the fire iron, and attacked the steam kettle, breaking its lid open, tipping it over so that the water spilled out and extinguished the hearth fire, then finally piercing its bottom for good measure.

Jalal yelled, "Nasruddin, you moron, why in Allah's name did you attack and ruin my water kettle?"

Nasruddin replied, gasping, "You have to kill these devils while they're little. Otherwise, they grow up to become terrible monsters. As it so happens, one of the huge mature ones almost killed me on my way here."

LONG DAY'S JOURNEY

Early one morning, Mullah Nasruddin was on the road when he entered an unfamiliar village. There he encountered a traveling scholar who appeared to be leaving town. He asked, "Where are you coming from, and where are you going?"

He replied derisively, "I am starting my journey — at the root of your testes!"

The Mullah answered, "Ah, so you have a long way to travel. By the time the sun sets, then, you will likely have arrived at the glans of my penis."

MIDDLE OF THE MAT

The Mullah was traveling with Faik and Hussein when they realized the three men would have to shelter overnight together in the cold. Faik suggested, "We should all buy a mat and a blanket together."

Nasruddin said, "I'll purchase the mat and share it with you, but not the blanket. You also must agree that I get to sleep in the middle between you two." So, he paid the other two for just his share of the mat.

Faik and Hussein could not obtain the mat without the Mullah's contribution but, thinking they would not share the cover with Nasruddin, they agreed. The three men bought the mat, and the other two obtained the blanket.

Nasruddin laid himself in the center of the mat and went to sleep. Now, if the other two wanted to share it, they had to sleep on either side of him. Then they realized that they could not tear the blanket so that each man could have his own. Thus Nasruddin got to enjoy the blanket without paying for it.

BURIAL GROUNDS OF POOR STRANGERS

Nasruddin was traveling down a road in a foreign land when he encountered a young woman washing clothes by a well. When she saw the Mullah passing by, she showed him her pussy and called out, "Old Mullah, tell me: where you come from, what do they call this?"

Nasruddin walked over to the well. Using a suggestive word, he answered, "By my Willie, I declare that that is the 'loveliest flower.'"

The woman said, "Why, Mullah, you're wrong! This is called 'the burial grounds of poor strangers.'"

"I understand perfectly," he replied. Nasruddin took a piece of white cloth from the woman, then he found a stick and tied it to his cock with the fabric wrapped around its length. Then he placed it on a washing stone in front of the woman and solemnly and loudly began reciting the Muslim prayer for the dead, *Vahdehu lâ şerike lehu.*

"Why, Mullah, what a strange act," said the woman. "What exactly is the meaning of this? Who has died that you mourn?"

Mullah cried, "Oh, woe to my poor departed friend! He is all alone! He has gone to God."

She pointed to his cock and asked, "Are you talking about that friend of yours in the cloth?"

"*Aman!* Surely you can tell," Mullah said, "that this is the funeral for my dear departed friend. Willie was a hardworking but penniless man, an unfortunate wanderer, a foreigner to these parts. See him all alone here, laid before you in a shroud. Without delay, we must carry this poor stranger to the burial grounds and inter him in his proper resting place."

The woman eagerly agreed, and Nasruddin removed the cloth and wood and prepared to enter her. Just as he was about to bury the corpse, she reached down and grabbed him by the balls. "Not so fast, Mullah," she said, and squeezed hard, "The big stranger is not all alone. Who are these big furry fellows, here?"

Nasruddin gasped, "They are the sons and heirs of the deceased who have carried Willie's body here. Please do not deny them the chance to attend their father's burial and pay their simple condolences."

MY REGULAR TURBAN

As the vicious despot Tamerlane and his troops approached the town in which Nasruddin lived, a group of village elders came to Nasruddin's house and awoke him.

Naked, the Mullah sleepily answered the door, and the terrified townspeople implored him to quickly do something to stop the tyrant from marching and rampaging through Akşehir.

Immediately Nasruddin took his bedsheets and wrapped them around his nearly bald head. When he finished, his headgear was as big as a wheel on a cart. Then, nude except for the turban, he mounted his little gray donkey and rode out to meet Tamerlane.

When Nasruddin approached Tamerlane, the shah exclaimed, "Mullah! What in the world are you wearing?"

"Please pardon me for my attire, your Highness," replied Nasruddin, yawning, "but this is just my nightcap. When I heard you were on your way here, I wanted to be sure to be first to welcome you. With no time to dress, I rushed from my bed wearing this instead of my regular turban. The turban that I usually wear during the day is even bigger and requires another cart to follow after me."

Tamerlane was so surprised and amused at the strange behavior and clothing of the Mullah that he decided to keep moving on.

THE COMPANY OF WOMEN

The Shah enjoyed spending excessive amounts of his time and fortune on his harem, cavorting day and night with his many wives, slaves, and servant women. His trusted confidant and advisor Mullah Nasruddin repeatedly advised him to restrain his appetite for the company of women. "Playing around so fool-ishly will doubtless sap all your strength and resources Inevitably, this wanton behavior bring you to an early and most unfortunate end."

At first, the Shah disregarded the Mullah's stern advice as regards his concubines and continued his lustful ways. Over time, however, the Shah began to comply with Nasruddin's directive and ignored his consorts.

One of the harem women, Zeynep, who was as smart as she was beautiful, was dismayed by her master's inattention. She went to him and asked, "You must tell me, my love: please explain why I have fallen out of your favor."

Upon learning the reason behind the Shah's recent change, she challenged him, "Present me to Nasruddin and tell him I will be his servant but not his slave. Trust me — I will teach that ridiculous old Mullah a lesson he won't easily forget."

As soon as the lovely young woman came to live in his house, Nasruddin took a keen interest in her. Every chance he got, when they were alone, he tried to have his way with her, but she steadfastly rebuked his efforts.

After several days of this cat-and-mouse game, Zeynep pretended to accede to his advances. She said, "I will let you touch me only under one condition. If you are truthful to me about your desire, then you must let me ride on your naked back as a sign of your submission."

Nasruddin had no problem whatsoever with this stipulation. He removed his shirt and offered his back to her, but it was not what she had in mind. She kicked him in the rear and cried, "Not so fast, you lecherous creep! It is not proper for a lady to ride without a saddle and whip."

As the Mullah trotted out to the stable to get the saddle and whip, Zeynep sent a messenger to run and bring the Shah there.

Nasruddin went out to the stable and put his horse's saddle on his back, then presented himself back to the vixen, offering her the whip. Again she kicked him and yelled, "Don't you know anything, you cretin? It isn't proper for a lady to ride unless her mount has a bridle in his mouth and has removed his trousers."

When Nasruddin returned, the woman mounted the naked man, settled into the saddle, grabbed the reins, and snapped the whip in the air. Zeynep then began riding her new pony boy around the house.

A few minutes later, the Shah burst in Nasruddin's house and witnessed the spectacle. He laughed and exclaimed, "Look at this! First, the Mullah admonishes me to restrain myself from my women, and now, here he is, behaving like an ass in hopes of fucking a beautiful lady. What has come over you, Nasruddin?"

Nasruddin stopped prancing around with the temptress on his back. He removed the harness and replied to the Shah, "What has come over me? I am simply trying to teach you an honest lesson: never let a woman make a jackass out of you as this bitch has done to me."

SMALL CONSOLATION

One day as Nasruddin was traveling, he met on the road a Turkman who halted him and asked, "Tell me, sir, are you a mullah?"

Nasruddin said, "Yes, I am."

The fellow clasped his hands and told him, "Our small tribe has no imam. Please come with me to our village, and you can serve our tribe as our spiritual leader."

Nasruddin agreed, and so the men continued on their journey. After they had walked for hours, they came to a crossroads, where they happened to meet another fellow. He asked the first Turkman, "Who is this man with you?"

He grabbed Nasruddin's arm, saying, "He is our beloved new imam. I'm taking him right now to my tribe, which has been without a religious leader for more than a year."

The second Turkman raised his voice, "You must surrender this mullah to us. My tribe hasn't had an imam in nine years." And he grabbed the mullah's other arm.

"Screw you, loser," said the first man, pulling hard on Nasruddin's arm. "We recruited him hours ago."

"Go fuck yourself, asshole," he replied, pulling the Mullah's arm in the other direction, "my tribe needs him more. Give him to us!"

As they argued, the men stretched the Mullah, jerking and wrenching his arms, for several minutes.

Finally, the second man pulled out a large knife and yelled, "Enough! Release him, or I'll slit his throat. That way, he'll be of no benefit to either your tribe or ours."

Nasruddin stood between them, trembling with fear.

The first man, to console the Mullah, assured him, "Don't worry, effendi — I swear, if he kills you, I'll go right to his house and murder his dog to avenge your death!"

FROM HELL TO PARADISE

In the days when Mullah Nasruddin was wandering as a penniless mendicant, he encountered a feeble but wealthy elderly woman who asked him, "You look like a holy man to me. Pray tell, sir, where are you coming from?"

"Why in Allah's name does it matter where I'm from?" he said. "But, since you asked, I'm from the deepest, darkest hole in Hell."

The lady's rheumy eyes filled with tears. as she asked, "Please, kindest Mullah, tell me truly: did you see my beloved dead son there?"

"Actually, as a matter of fact, I happened to see your son not long ago," replied the Mullah. "Sadly, he died a despised debtor, and for that, he was denied entry to Paradise. The last I saw of your son, he was selling beans at the gates of Hell."

The woman sobbed, "*Aiii*, what a horrible fate! Do you happen to know the amount of his remaining debt?"

"Two hundred silver coins," replied Nasruddin, settling on a reasonable sum. "Your son's wife is already in Paradise awaiting him. But your wayward son can only get there if he has repaid the thousand silver pieces."

The woman inquired, "And when do you intend to return to that wretched place?"

"As soon as the sun rises, if not before."

The hopeful old woman turned out to be the wife of a corrupt constable who lived nearby but happened to be out of the house. She asked the Mullah to wait there while she hurried back home, got out her husband's hidden stash of stolen goods and bribery loot, counted out three hundred silver pieces in a sack, then rushed back.

"Here then, take three hundred coins to give to my son. You must free him from that despicable debt! Run and do not cause further delay in the matter!"

"Fine, I'm heading out in just a minute or two," the Mullah said.

The woman bade the Mullah to wait once more and hurried back home, retrieved a pair of clean underwear, then went to the Mullah and gave it to him, saying, "Please sir, be so kind as to take this to my child as well, since you are going to see him anyway."

"No doubt he'll appreciate it, good woman. And now most certainly it is time for me to depart."

The woman went home, where she met her husband, who had just returned as well. She told him the great good news, "My dear, I have just this morning received word of our dear departed son. Since he can only come to Paradise for the low price of three hundred silver coins, I've given it to him to take to our son so he can pay his debts and get the hell out of the Netherworld."

"Hold on — who is this 'him' to whom you gave three hundred silver coins? What grifter informed you about this fare from Hell to Paradise?"

She replied, "Actually, he was a very nice mullah I met on the street. The good man assured me that he was returning directly to Hell to pay our son's debt."

"You don't say. Did you happen to notice which direction the mullah was heading to go to Hell?"

The woman pointed south. Immediately the man mounted his horse and set out to locate the Mullah.

Meanwhile, Nasruddin had reached a mill at the edge of the next town and stopped to catch his breath. When from a distance he saw a man riding a horse directly toward him, he ducked into the mill. He breathlessly said to the miller, "Brother, I have come to warn you — leave this very minute and hide!"

The miller said, "What in Allah's name are you talking about, Mullah?"

Nasruddin pointed and said, "Do you see the man who approaches us on horseback from the north? He is a crooked, violent cop from the next town who comes to arrest you for some past misdeed! You should prepare to go to prison — or you may even be hanged."

Confused and frightened, the miller asked, "Really? What did I do to deserve this? What should I do now? You must save me!"

Nasruddin snapped his fingers and said, "I've got a plan, but we must act fast. Quickly, strip and put on my clothes. I'll put on yours. Give me your fez for my turban. Now, quickly — climb up that tall tree and stay there, and be silent! He'll be here at any moment. Somehow I'll figure out how to get rid of him for you."

No sooner had the two completed exchanging clothes, and the miller was hiding in the tree, the woman's husband rode up to the mill.

He first noticed a fellow dressed like a miller and asked him, "Miller, did you see the mullah who just came by here? Which way did he go?"

Nasruddin, who was pretending to be busy with milling work, nodded toward the tree. The bekche dismounted and quietly approached the tree. As he got closer and could look up into the branches, he saw there the alleged mullah in his robes. So as not to get his fancy shoes and clothes dirty, he quickly disrobed, then jumped up and headed up the tree.

As soon as he cop reached the branch below the miller, the Mullah grabbed his clothes and mounted the horse. "Hey, numbnuts!" he shouted, while he rode off. "Have you not realized who I am?"

As the two victims of the Mullah's guile descended the tree, the miller screamed obscenities at the cop until the near-naked man left the mill and walked home in shame.

He finally returned, and his wife asked eagerly, "Tell me, what happened? Where is your horse? Why are you just wearing your underwear? What happened when you met up with the nice mullah who's bailing out our son?"

The constable coughed and said, "I caught up with the mullah at long last. And what he told you about our son is the absolute truth. So, I gave him my clothes to take to our boy, and for his thoughtful service to our son and us, I offered my horse to the Mullah, to speed him on his long journey to the Underworld."

CLIMATE CHANGE

Nasruddin was preaching one day at the mosque in the town of Sivrihisar. He declared, "Oh, true believers! Bismillah, I have discovered a great secret." Then he fell silent.

Someone asked, "Please tell us, Mullah, what is this awesome hidden knowledge you have come to share with us?"

"I have found . . . the climate here in Sivrihisar to be precisely the same as my home, back in Karahisar!"

"How did you come to that conclusion, Mullah?"

"You see, I've noticed at home that my limp cock clings to my balls, and the very thing has happened here too. Therefore I deduce that the weather must be the same in both places."

THE PROPHET'S TRADITION

When Nasruddin was an old man, Ahmet asked, "Father, do you think any of the sayings of the Prophet as being especially meaningful to you?"

The Mullah replied, "Once a very long time ago, my father, peace be upon him, spoke of a brief Tradition of the Prophet, which his mother's father had told him, and which he believed that nobody else had ever heard."

Ahmet was excited at the prospect of hearing an untold Tradition and said, "Please, Father, I beseech you to tell me these holy words of the Prophet."

"If I recall correctly," Nasruddin began, "that Al-Rabi heard a Tradition from Ibn Abbas, who heard it from the Prophet Muhammad, who said, 'There are two personality traits which are not seen in a person until he is a true believer.' "

Ahmet leaned forward to listen to his father utter the Prophet's sacred words.

Nasruddin sat back and said, "Sad to say, my father had forgotten one of the personality traits — and I can not remember the other."

No translation

The esteemed Mullah was sent on a vital and delicate diplomatic mission to Kurdistan to accompany the ambassador and a translator.

Once they arrived, the Kurdish leaders' interpreter announced that they had prepared a feast for the delegation and invited the dignitaries to join them. The Turks put on their finery and went to the dining hall. They were given seats of honor, and the banquet proceeded.

After the sumptuous meal, the esteemed Kurdish commander stood to formally address the group, and the room quieted down in anticipation. Nasruddin had flatulence and let out a loud, long fart.

The ambassador's face turned beet red. He said, "You farted, Nasruddin, and have thus disgraced all of Turkey!"

Nasruddin gave a small shrug and a weak smile. "But these are all Kurds here. How in the world would they understand a Turkish fart?"

The power of chalk

In Konya, a bekche caught Nasruddin chalking a political slogan on the wall of a building, and dragged him to jail. His queer appearance and irrational behavior led to his being certified insane, and so he was transferred to the regional mental hospital.

The insane asylum, of course, was filled with a frightening variety of depraved idiots and perverted lunatics. As soon as the Mullah entered the courtyard, the inmates crowded around him as if he were carrion and they were buzzards circling, ready to land. He could smell their soiled clothes and foul breath as they circled him.

Nasruddin held up his hands to repel the sociopaths and shouted, "Stop, you fiends!" He pulled from his pocket the offensive piece of chalk. "Stand back, or else," he hissed, brandishing the chalk as if it were a knife.

The crazies halted in their spots.

Moving quickly, Nasruddin drew a line across the courtyard dividing the inmates evenly into two groups. Standing at the end of the line, he announced, "Pay attention, people! Here are the *new rules*. Now, first, does everyone see clearly the chalk line that I drew on the ground?"

The demented inmates nodded and grunted their mutual assent.

"Good. That's the line. So, the only other rule of the new game is simple: on my call, all of you must jump under that line. The first man who makes it under wins this chalk and gets to make up the next game." He walked to the periphery of the two teams, saying, "I will say when to begin. Ready, set, go."

The casualties were severe as both teams went berserk and threw themselves repeatedly at the line and each other.

Nasruddin was released. Nobody was quite sure whether it was because they could not allow further injuries of the inmates, or because his clever resourcefulness proved his sanity.

FULL MOON AND NEW MOON

Mullah Nasruddin traveled to Kabul and was picked up by the corrupt local cops on the false charge of being a Persian spy. The brought him before the Afghan sovereign in court, where he tried to convince the monarch that he was no spy at all, but just a respectable emissary of his country.

The King addressed Nasruddin, "Since a true emissary must travel widely, and you appear to be a learned man of wide experience, let me ask you: what do you think of me and my reign of the country?"

Nasruddin enthusiastically replied, "I would compare your Majesty favorably to the full moon, which is most mature and gives the most light."

"That is a kind comparison, indeed," responded the king. "But Mullah, if I am the full moon, pray tell, what is Padishah Akbar, your king?"

Nasruddin replied, "I would say that Akbar is more like the new moon."

Though his response pleased the Afghan king, Nasruddin knew that the genuine Turkish spies in the Afghan court would immediately report his conversation back to Akbar.

Upon his return, Nasruddin appeared in court and Akbar confronted him. "Is it true that you described the Afghan ruler as being like the full moon?" Nasruddin nodded. "And is it correct that you said that I, your sovereign, resemble the new moon?"

Nasruddin said, "Yes, your Majesty, that is also true."

"Were you thus not insulting your monarch and praising the king of a neighboring country?"

"Of course not, your Majesty," Nasruddin answered. "Only a nitwit like the Afghan king would be flattered by such a comparison."

"Explain yourself," demanded Akbar.

"When I said that he was like the full moon, I meant that he had already achieved the peak of his powers and that his reign and influence would only diminish with time. Indeed, it was clear to me that his future looked bleak."

Akbar smiled and motioned for Nasruddin to continue.

"I spoke of you as being like the new moon, whose potential is vast, whose brilliance is in ascent, and whose glorious golden years are soon coming. Nobody with any sense would have construed it otherwise. Perhaps some of your bumbling spies — I mean, other emissaries — misinterpreted my words on purpose. I would be very suspicious of these persons, my liege."

"Advice well considered," said Akbar, as he proudly rewarded Nasruddin a bag of gold for his loyalty and diplomacy.

THE GREATER FOOL

Once while Mullah Nasruddin was traveling peaceably on donkeyback through Foolland, he passed two local fellows trudging along on foot. Nasruddin greeted them, saying only, "Good morning."

As the Mullah kept riding along past the men, the first fool stopped and remarked, "I'm wondering . . . why did that fellow speak to me, and not to you?"

The other fool retorted, "You self-centered moron, it was me he was addressing, not you. Why do you always think it's about you?"

It took less than a minute before the two were pushing and shoving each other. They were about to come to blows when one held up his hand and said, "I know — let's ask him!" So they chased after the Mullah, who was trying to ease out of the skirmish and down the road with his little gray donkey and his serenity intact.

"Wait, Mullah! You must settle our dispute: to which one of us were you saying 'Good morning'?"

Nasruddin urged Karakacan to keep moving as he replied to the men, "All that I said was: 'Good morning' and I was only addressing the greater fool."

"Well, clearly, that means me," declared the first fellow.

"Nonsense, you pigheaded nitwit, not you! Of course, he meant that I'm the greater one," asserted the second.

"You worthless piece of crap, it's obvious to anyone that I'm a far superior fool than you could ever aspire to be, in every way."

And so the two fools continued swearing and exchanging slaps and curses in the middle of the road, raising a cloud of dust that became smaller and smaller as the little gray donkey Karakacan carried Mullah Nasruddin far, far away, until he could no longer hear or see the fools anymore, toward the sanctuary of his home.

Glossary

ai vai	alas!
'Al-Rabi	disciple of Muhammad's uncle, Ibn Abbas
Akşehir	village in south-central Turkey; literally, "white plain"
Allah	primary Arabic name for the Deity
aman	woe is me!
baklava	flaky pastry made with honey, cinnamon, and nuts
bekche	town watchman; constable
caliph	supreme ruler
dervish	Sufi ascetic
dinar	Persian currency
djinn	jinni, ghost
effendi	mister, sir: scholastic or official title; term of respect among equals
hajj	pilgrimage to Mecca, which every able-bodied Muslim is required to complete
halvah	sweetmeat made of sesame
hammam	Turkish bathhouse
hammamji	bathhouse attendant
Ibn Abbas	paternal uncle and companion to Muhammad
imam	prayer leader in mosque; Muslim leader
Insh'allah	God willing; I hope so
Islam	monotheistic religion articulated by the Quran

Kaaba	cube-shaped building in Mecca; most sacred site in Islam
Karahisar	town in Denizli, southwest Turkey
Konya	city in Anatolia, central Turkey
Malatya	city in central Turkey
Mecca	city in Saudi Arabia, a pilgrimage site for all Muslims
mescit	small mosque, often without a minaret or dome
minaret	mosque spire, usually with an onion-shaped or conical crown
mosque	Islamic house of worship
muezzin	Islamic cantor who calls the faithful to prayer five times a day
Muhammad	founder of Islam; the prophetic author of the Quran
mullah	learned Islamic cleric acting as judge, priest, and teacher
Muslim	adherent to Islam
namaz	Islamic divine worship, daily recitals of praise with prostrations
Nasruddin	name meaning "victory of religion"
Quran	Mohammedan holy book; literally, "the recitation"
Ramadan	Islamic month of fasting from dawn until sunset
sadir	couch in a hammam
salaam	hello; peace; greeting with folded hands
shah	king of Persia
sheikh	tribal or village elder; Muslim officiant
Shkodër	Town in Albania
Sivrihisar	Nasruddin birthplace in Turkey
Sufi	adherent to Sufism, mystical branch of Islam
Tamerlane	despotic ruler of the 14th Century

Sources

Al-Amily, Hussain Mohammed, compiler & editor. *The Book of Arabic Wisdom: Proverbs & anecdotes.* Northampton, Mass.: Interlink Books, 2004.

Ashliman, D. L. 2001. *Nasreddin Hodja: Tales of the Turkish trickster.* University of Pittsburgh <www.pitt.edu/~dash/hodja.html>, accessed 8/1/01.

Barnham, Henry D., translator. *Tales of Nasr-ed-din Khoja.* London: Nisbet & Co., 1923. Foreword, Sir Valentine Chirol.

Başgöz, İlhan. "A Thematic Analysis of Hodja Stories in Historical Perspective." In *I, Hodja Nasreddin, Never Shall I Die,* ed. İlhan Başgöz, 1-83. Bloomington: Indiana University Turkish Studies Series, 1998.

Birant, Mehmet Ali, compiler. *Nasreddin Hodja.* Ece Birant Sevil, translator. Ömer Dinçer Kiliç, illustrator. Ankara: Egitim Gereçcleri, 1994.

Boratav, Pertev Nailî. *Nasreddin Hoca.* Istanbul: Kırmızı Yayınları, 1995, 2006. In Turkish.

———. "The Turkish, the Muslim, and the Universal in Nasreddin Hoca Stories." In *I, Hodja Nasreddin, Never Shall I Die,* ed. İlhan Başgöz, 1-83. Bloomington: Indiana University Turkish Studies Series, 1998.

———. "Nasreddin Hoca Stories from Pertev Boratov." Translated by İlhan Başgöz. In *I, Hodja Nasreddin, Never Shall I Die,* ed. İlhan Başgöz, 1-83. Bloomington: Indiana University Turkish Studies Series, 1998.

Burrill, Kathleen Ruth Frances. 1957. *The Nasreddin Hoja stories.* New York: Columbia University Library, Special Collections. Ph.D dissertation. In Arabic, Turkish, and English.

Bushnaq, Inea, translator & editor. "Famous Fools and Rascals: Stories of Djuha and his kind," pp. 254–280 in her *Arab Folktales.* New York: Pantheon Fairy Tale & Folklore Library, 1986.

Calvino, Italo. *Italian Folk Tales*. Translated by George Martin. San Diego / New York / London: Harcourt, Inc., 1980.

Chukru, Kemaleddin. *Vie de Nasreddine Hodja*. Istanbul: Librarie Kaanat, [n.d.: 1931?]. Illustrated, Ömer Nuri, &c. In French.

Crane, Thomas Frederick. *Italian Popular Tales*. Cambridge, Mass.: Riverside Press, [1885] reprint 2010. Giufà stories, pp. 288–303.

Gűrkaş, Hakkı. *Nasreddin Hodja and the Akşehir Festival: Invention of a Festive Tradition and Transfigurations of a Trickster, from Bukhara to Brussels*. Ph.D dissertation. West Lafayette, Ind.: Purdue University, 2008.

Husain, Shahrukh. *The Wisdom of Mulla Nasruddin*. New Delhi: Scholastic, 2006. Illustrated, Shilpa Ranade.

Husseini, Khaled. *The Kite Runner*. New York: Riverhead Books, 2003. A novel.

Jamnia, Ali, translator. *Tales of Nasrudin: Keys to enlightenment*. San Rafael, Calif.: Sophia Perennis, 2006.

Jayyusi, Salma Khadra, editor. *Tales of Juha: Classic Arab folk humor*. Northampton, Mass.: Interlink Books, 2007. Translated, Matthew Sorenson, Faisal Khadra & Christopher Tingley.

Kabacali, Alpay. *Nasreddin Hodja*. Istanbul: Net Turiskik Yayinlar, 1992. Illustrated, Fatîh M. Durmus.

Karabas, Seyfi. "The Use of Eroticism in Nasreddin Hoca Anecdotes." In *Western Folklore* 49 : 3, pp. 299–305. Long Beach, Calif.: Western States Folklore Society, July 1990.

Kelsey, Alice Geer. *Once the Hodja*. New York: David McKay Co., 1943. Illustrated, Frank Dobias.

———. *Once the Mullah: Persian Folk Tales*. New York, Toronto, & London: Longmans, Green & Co., 1958. Illustrated, Kurt Werth.

Kúnos, Ignácz. *Turkish Fairy Tales and Folktales*. LaVergne, Tenn.: Kessinger Legacy Series, 1896, reprint 2010. Translated, R. Nisbet Bain & Celia Levetus. Illustrated, Celia Levetus.

Leach, Maria. *Noodles, Nitwits, and Numskulls*. Cleveland: World Publishing, 1961. Illustrated, Kurt Werth.

Legman, Gershon. *The Horn Book: Studies in Erotic Folklore and Bibliography.* New Hyde Park, N.Y.: University Books, 1964.

————. *Rationale of the Dirty Joke: An Analysis of Sexual Humor.* First Series. New York: Grove Press, 1968.

————. *No Laughing Matter. Rationale of the Dirty Joke: An Analysis of Sexual Humor.* Second Series. New York: Bell Press, 1975.

Levett, Yoram, collector & editor. *Hakmut Nasaruddin.* Jerusalem: Beit Ho-tzaah Elishair, 1982. Illustrated, A. Nikolaiv. In Hebrew.

MacDonald, Margaret Read. *The Storyteller's Sourcebook: a subject, title, and motif index to folklore collections for children.* 1st edition. Detroit, Mich.: Gale Group, 1982.

MacDonald, Margaret Read, & Brian W. Sturm. *The Storyteller's Sourcebook: a subject, title, and motif index to folklore collections for children, 1983-1999.* Detroit, Mich.: Gale Group, 2001.

Mahfuzdur, Her Hakki. *202 Jokes of Nasreddin Hodja.* Tepebaşı, Istanbul: Galeri Minyatür, Minyatür Yayinlari No. 1b, [n.d.]. Illustrated, uncredited.

Marzolph, Ulrich, collector & editor. *Nasreddin Hodsca: 666 wahre Geschichten.* Munchen: C.H. Beck, 2006. In German.

Nesin, Aziz. *The Tales of Nasrettin Hoca.* Istanbul: Dost Yayinlari, revised edition 1994. Translated, Talât Sait Halman. Illustrated, Zeki Fındıkoğlu.

Özdemir, Nebi. M. Angela Roome, translator. *The Philosopher's Philosopher, Nasreddin Hodja.* Ankara: Republic of Turkey, Ministry of Culture and Tourism. Handbook Series, 2011.

Issue theme: "The Fool." In *Parabola: Myth, tradition, and the search for meaning* 26: 3. Denville, N.J.: The Society for the Study of Myth and Tradition, Fall 2001.

Sawhney, Clifford. *The Funniest Tales of Mullah Nasruddin: The wittiest stories of the world's best-loved jester.* New Delhi: Unicorn Press, 2009. Illustrated, uncredited.

Schiff, Jeremy. *Hodja Stories.* Ramat Gan, Israel: <http://u.cs.biu.ac.il/ ~schiff/ Hodja/>, accessed 8/1/01.

Serwer-Bernstein, Blanche L. *In the Tradition of Moses and Mohammed: Jewish and Arab folktales.* Northvale, N.J.: Jason Aronson, 1994.

Shah, Idries. *The Exploits of the Incomparable Mulla Nasrudin*. New York: Arkana/Penguin, 1966. Illustrated, Richard Williams.

————. *The Pleasantries of the Incredible Mulla Nasrudin*. New York: Arkana / Penguin, 1968, 1993. Illustrated, Richard Williams & Errol Le Cain.

————. *The Subtleties of the Inimitable Mulla Nasrudin*. New York: Arkana/Penguin, 1973.

————. *Las Hazañas del Incomparable Mulá Nasrudín*. Barcelona / Bueños Aires: Paidos Orientalia, 1990. *Exploits*, in Spanish.

————. *The World of Nasrudin*. London: Octagon Press, 2003.

Solovyov, Leonid. *Disturber of the Peace: The tale of Hodja Nasreddin*. Thornhill, Ontario, Canada: Translit Publishing, 2009. Translated, Michael Karpelson. A novel.

————. *Hodja Nasar a-Din*. Translated, Spiryat ben Chaskin. Tel-Aviv: Am Oved Publishers, 1968. In Hebrew.

Stevens, E. S., translator & editor. *Folktales of Iraq*. Mineola, N.Y.: Dover Publications, 1913, 2006.

Suresha, Ron J. *The Uncommon Sense of the Immortal Mullah Nasruddin: Stories, jests, and donkey tales of the beloved Persian folk hero*. 2nd revised edition. New Milford, Conn.: Bear Bones Books, 2017.

Thompson, Stith. *Motif-Index of Folk Literature*. Vols. 1–6. Bloomington: Indiana University Press, 1955–1958.

Walker, Barbara. *Watermelons, Walnuts, and the Wisdom of Allah: And other tales of the Hoca*. Lubbock: Texas Tech University Press, 1991. Illustrated, Harold Berson.

Wesselski, Albert. *Der Hodscha Nasreddin*. Charleston, S.C.: Bibliolife, 1911, reprint 2011. In German.

Yörenç, Kemal. *The Best Anecdotes of Nasreddin Hoca*. Istanbul: Aksit Kültür Turizm Sanat Ajans Ticaret, 1997. Illustrated, Kemal Yörenç.

Acknowledgments

This book is dedicated to the memory of Robin Williams.

Thanks to Toby Johnson for his invaluable design and production assistance, and to cover illustrator Jaxinto.

I am indebted to the Connecticut Storytelling Center in New London, and especially to its director, Ann Shapiro.

Many stories are sourced from texts published in languages in which I am not fluent, including French, German, Hebrew, Hindi, Spanish, and Turkish. Credit is due to Google Translate and Bing Translator in regard to rendering German, Spanish, and French sources. Yet for Turkish and other languages there could be no substitute for the guidance of a native speaker or professional translator, and this work has been aided immeasurably with the assistance of Mehmet Ali Şahin, who reviewed Turkish tales presented by Burrill and Boratav; to Steven Packard, who reviewed and clarified stories in German presented by Marzolph and Wesselski; and to Meir Amiel for translations from Hebrew.

I'm grateful for readers Ralph Seligman-Courtois and David Midyette. Thanks additionally to Jeff Shaumeyer, David Juhren, Daniel M. Jaffe, Joel Perry, and Dave O'Neal.

To my yoga teachers and friends: thank you, and bless you. Namasté.

These comedians, satirists, and pundits have inspired me while working on this material and deserve a tip of the fez: Bruce Vilanch, Scott Thompson, Stephanie Miller, John Fugelsang, Marc Maron, Judy Gold, Kate Clinton, Dave Chappelle, Zach Galifianakis, Al Franken, Dean Obeidallah, Rachel Maddow, Cenk Uygur, and Bill Maher.

Finally, I offer my most heartfelt gratitude to Rocco, without whose espousal and embrace this work could not have been accomplished. *Ti voglio bene assai.*

About the Author

Ron J. Suresha, an award-winning author whose spiritual travels have included pilgrimages to India, Israel, and Istanbul, has been acquainted with the Turkish folk hero Mullah Nasruddin since his childhood in Detroit, Michigan. During the 1980s, while working as a typographer in various cities around the United States, he lived in an ashram (residential yoga community) where he learned hatha yoga, calligraphy, and many Nasruddin stories. For much of the 1990s, he worked as a freelance proofreader and production editor for publishers of Eastern religious and spiritual books.

Suresha's published nonfiction works include: a self-published beverage recipé book, *Mugs o' Joy: Delicious Hot Drinks* (1998, reprinted 2013); an acclaimed 2002 book on the worldwide gay and bisexual men's Bear subculture, *Bears on Bears: Interviews & Discussions* (2nd revised edition, Bear Bones Books, 2018); and two anthologies, *Bi Men: Coming Out* (edited with Pete Chvany, Haworth/Routledge, 2006), and *Bisexual Perspectives on the Life and Work of Alfred C. Kinsey* (Routledge, 2010), both finalists for the Lambda Literary Award. He also authored with Scott McGillivray a 2012 pictorial book with essays, *Fur: The Love of Hair* (Bruno Gmünder), winner of a Rainbow Book Award. Suresha additionally writes and edits fiction under the pseudonym R. Jackson.

The author, who resides with his husband in central western Connecticut, is the founder and publisher of Bear Bones Books. Discover much more online at:

www.RonSuresha.com
www.MullahNasruddin.com
www.BearBonesBooks.com

Also by Ron J. Suresha

The Uncommon Sense of the Immortal Mullah Nasruddin:
Stories, Jests, and Donkey Tales of the Beloved Persian Folk Hero

AN ANNE IZARD STORYTELLERS' CHOICE AWARD WINNER
A STORYTELLING WORLD HONOR BOOK

"These hilarious, and at times, ribald folk tales of the Turkish wise fool take the reader to another time and place, and share the spiritual lessons of Nasruddin. . . . The teaching stories included in this volume help to build bridges between cultures by exemplifying Arabic wisdom and universal human humor." — Ann Shapiro, Executive Director, Connecticut Storytelling Center

"A fine pick and very highly recommended." — *Midwest Book Review*

"Identifies the real strength of Nasruddin's stories in context to world literature and story performance, that is, its power to build bridges between cultures. The point of these stories is to speak to the audience in the language and metaphors that are familiar." — *Storytelling, Self, Society*

"A valuable source-book of little-known material from a not very well-known culture. . . . Suresha's efforts in recreating such a 'serious' collection of humorous stories are to be appreciated." — *The Humorous Times: Newsletter of the International Center for Humor Studies*

"A contemporary reworking of the stories fit for a general audience. . . . The book has maintained the direct, unadorned style that is a hallmark of folk tales. . . . A delightful break from the everyday world for an hour or two." — *Green Man Review*

Softcover ISBN: 978-1-59021-175-5

Also available from Bear Bones Books as an Audible.com audiobook narrated by Ted Brooks.

Made in the USA
San Bernardino,
CA